DO YOUR OWN
GARDEN STONEWORK

DO YOUR OWN GARDEN STONEWORK

by Geoff Hamilton

London.
W. FOULSHAM & CO. LTD
New York · Toronto · Capetown · Sydney

W. FOULSHAM & COMPANY LIMITED
Yeovil Road, SLOUGH, Berkshire SL1 4JH

ISBN 0-572-01374-4
© W. Foulsham & Co. Ltd. 1981 and 1986

Designed by Stonecastle Graphics

Photographs facing pages 32 and 33 are by courtesy of
S. MARSHALL & SONS LTD of HALIFAX
Photographs facing pages 64 and 65 are by courtesy of the
CEMENT & CONCRETE ASSOCIATION

Printed and bound in Great Britain
at The Bath Press, Avon

Contents

Gardens are there to be used, so they need a paved area for sitting out in all seasons and enjoying the fresh air.

Introduction

Throughout civilized man's history, stone, brick or concrete have been essential to his way of life. And, though some of the materials may have changed over the years, and building techniques have developed, we rely as much on them today as ever we did. Indeed, more so. Perhaps the day may come when metal and plastics take the place of more traditional materials, but that day is certainly not in the foreseeable future.

There must be very few gardens that do not sport a concrete driveway, a paved path or a patio for sitting out and enjoying the fresh air. Gardens are there to be *used*, not just in the summer, but also for that near half-year when our climate makes grass and soil inhospitable.

So most gardens will need a hard-standing for the car, a dry path alongside the washing line or a paved area where one can sit in the sunshine, eat out on warmer days or entertain one's friends to a barbecue.

As the need for housing becomes more acute, gardens are getting smaller, and sites more scarce. This inevitably results in 'difficult' gardens, where perhaps the land slopes sharply away from or towards the house. Then, the only solution is to build retaining walls and steps, and to landscape the garden into a series of flat, usable terraces. Properly done, this sort of garden can become a far more interesting and attractive feature than one built entirely on the flat.

In completely flat gardens, some sort of feature may be required to add height to an otherwise uninteresting vista. A raised bed, a brick flower-box or even a stone seat can make just that feature that makes all the difference.

This book sets out to provide the basic information necessary for the 'do-it-yourselfer' to tackle his own patio, driveway, retaining wall, or indeed any stonework project with the exception of pools and rock gardens. That's a subject for a book on its own.

To the gardener just starting from scratch, all this 'hard' landscaping may seem a daunting proposition. All that concrete to mix, and those heavy slabs to hump about. Well, in all honesty, it *is* going to be hard work. There are not many short cuts and, unless you do the job properly, you are wasting your time. But, once you get into it, I can almost guarantee that you'll find it an absorbing and highly satisfying job. A chance to create a thing of beauty that you'll be able to enjoy for the rest of your life. Because, done properly, a stone patio, a brick wall or a concrete driveway *will* last a lifetime. And it will add more than its cost to the value of your house.

1 Planning

Before you dig out a shovelful of soil or mix a barrowload of concrete, give your new project long and serious thought. Bear in mind that your handiwork will be there for a long, long time. You *must* get it right first time.

Start by taking a few walks around your new 'estate' to get the feel of the place. Make sure you know which parts of the garden are likely to be in full sun and which will be shaded for part of the day. If you are building a patio, for example, decide what times of the day you are most likely to use it, and ensure that at those times it will be bathed in sunshine if you are a sun-lover, or that it will be in the shade if you find the heat oppressive.

Think about the garden as a whole. It is no good, for instance, siting the washing line in a spot where the clean sheets will flap all over the roses. That does neither of them any good. Don't build that decorative wall to mask the dustbins to the windward of your sitting-out area, and don't hide the coal-bunker at the far end of the garden where you'll freeze to death fetching the coal on a wintry night.

Above all, discuss your ideas in depth with your wife or your husband. Two heads are always better than one.

When you really feel that you know the site, it's time to start committing a few ideas to paper. Again, there is no rush. You almost certainly won't get it right first time.

Measure up the rough size and shape of the plot, and draw it out on a sheet of paper. There is no need at this stage to be too accurate. Start by drawing in the essentials. Certainly you'll want a hard path leading to both front and rear doors, you may need a hard-standing for the car, and this can generally only be put in one place, and most families will need somewhere to dry the washing. You should consider a spot for the dustbin, and you may need to provide a path to the rear gate.

Even with these factors, there is room for manoeuvre and a chance to make an attractive feature. A brick path winding round the edge of the lawn, for instance, will look attractive, fulfil a useful function, and make the maintenance of the grass much easier too. Even the place where the rubbish is left for the dustman can be made to look attractive by hiding it with a decorative wall, perhaps covered with roses or sweet-smelling honeysuckle. You'll soon begin to realize that this is one of the most exciting stages of the whole operation.

If you are building paths or walls across the garden, try not to cut it into strips. This will only serve to reduce the apparent size of the garden. Often, by building in some curves, you can actually make the garden seem to increase in size.

1. By building some curves into the garden, it can be made to look larger than it really is.

2. A corner patio is often more useful than the conventional long, thin strip at the back of the house.

Of course, at this stage you will also have to take some account of cost. But don't let the thought of your bank manager's apoplexy prevent you from *planning* your project, even if you can't afford it all at once. If the job is properly planned, there is no reason at all why you should not complete it in stages. But it should be planned as a whole at the outset. There is nothing worse than the garden which is planned piecemeal. It will always look as though half of it has been an afterthought, and will never come together as a cohesive entity.

As well as thinking about the aesthetic appeal of a feature, you should also consider its usefulness. If, for example, you wish to build a patio, make sure that it is made to a usable shape. The long thin strip outside the back of the house, so beloved of all builders apparently, is virtually useless. Try putting a table and half-a-dozen chairs round it for an alfresco meal, and the poor chap nearest the edge will be in constant danger of falling off! Using exactly the same amount of paving, the patio could be built at one end of the house in a square, triangular or semicircular shape, to provide a much more accessible area.

But, even if the bank balance is becoming stretched, beware of skimping. That is the greatest folly of them all. Narrow paths always look mean and ugly and, though it may seem a paradox, make the whole garden shrink. There is no real rule of thumb for determining size, except that the separate features should be in scale with the rest of the garden.

Every garden should be a green and pleasant place, and however hard you try, 'hard' landscaping will tend to look unnatural. So allow plenty of scope for softening it with plants. A large area of paving can be broken up and 'softened' by leaving areas in it unpaved to grow plants. Just by cutting off the corner of a slab, filling the hole with soil and planting an alpine plant or a prostrate conifer, you will add interest and colour. And the patio will start to become an integral part of the garden scheme rather than standing out like a sore thumb.

3. Leave some spaces so that 'hard' areas of paving can be softened by judicious planting.

Similar holes can be left in walls, so that a few plants can be poked in to soften the hard lines. If you need to build double walls, the top can be left unfilled, so that it can be planted and brought to life.

It is essential, too, at the planning stage to think about levels, and this is particularly so if the garden is on a slope.

If the patio is to be sited next to the house wall, it *must* finish at least two courses below the damp-proof course. Failure to do this will result in water creeping through the wall to the inside of the house, and destroying plaster and wallpaper. A daunting thought indeed.

It must also slope away from the house so that rain water runs away from the wall. This may mean that a retaining wall may need to be built at the edge of the patio, and this must be planned at the outset.

You may also have to think about drainage, especially if the garden slopes towards the house. If the patio is

4. Wide paths can also be planted to 'soften' the hard lines while still retaining their usefulness.

enclosed with a retaining wall, there will be nowhere for the water to get away. And after a heavy storm, there could be a lot of water on a large area of paving. Naturally, the drains must be built before the paving is laid, so they too must be planned right from the start.

With all these factors to be borne in mind, even the best of planners take a long time and make dozens of rough drawings. It is well worth it in the end.

Finally, bear in mind that a garden is an intensely personal thing. It is a living manifestation of your own ideas and your own personality. No-one can advise you on that. If it suits *you*, then it is right. You cannot get that sort of inspiration from other people or from a book. Not even this one.

2 Choosing

With so many different types of paving and walling available, the prospective buyer is often faced with a knotty problem. Of course, price will make a big difference, but this should not, if at all possible, be allowed to dominate your choice. It is generally better to settle for nothing less than the best material for the job, even if it means either delaying the work for a while, or completing it in stages. Remember that the feature will be there for life, and the cost will certainly be recouped if the house is sold. Above all, you have to live with it and *enjoy* it, so the first criterion should be to choose a material that is pleasing to your eye.

There are other more practical considerations to be borne in mind too. If, for example, your proposed patio is in a situation or of a design that will entail a lot of cutting of slabs, it is important to buy paving that will cut easily and cheaply with a chisel. The hire of a stone saw for more difficult slabs will increase the cost of the job considerably.

If you are laying a path that is to be continually in the shade, moss and algae will almost certainly form on the surface, making it very slippery. This can be very dangerous indeed, especially to visitors, who may be unaware of the conditions. In this case, slabs with a non-slip surface are absolutely essential if nasty accidents are to be avoided.

The size of slabs may be an important consideration too. If, for example, you intend to pave a path 1m(3ft) wide, it would be quite impracticable to buy slabs 60cm(2ft) wide. That would mean that every other slab would have to be cut in half. A time-consuming and unrewarding job.

The thickness of the slabs you buy must also be taken

into account. If you intend to run the car over them, let alone the tanker that fills the oil storage tank, they *must* be no less than 5cm(2in) thick. Anything thinner will almost certainly crack under the weight of a vehicle. In this case, insist on slabs that have been machine pressed as opposed to those that have been moulded. Pressed slabs are much stronger.

If you are simply building a patio or a path that will be used only for pedestrian traffic, your choice is much wider. Here, thinner slabs are quite satisfactory, and much lighter. This means that, provided you choose slabs of a reasonable size, you will be able to handle them yourself and will not have to rely on help from friends or neighbours. Generally speaking, a fit, able-bodied man not plagued with back troubles should be able to handle slabs 60cm × 60cm × 5cm (2ft × 2ft × 2in) all day without too much problem. If you're not used to that sort of work, take it easy and don't try to do too much at once. That may be difficult, because once you start, you'll certainly want to carry on. But, the following morning, you'll know you've done it!

Bricks, must be chosen with a view to the job they have to do. First *never* use common fletton bricks in the garden, they are made for inside walls and will flake right from the very first frost.

Sand-faced flettons or stock bricks can be used in the garden for walling, but they should not be used for brick paving. They are made for situations where water will run off them immediately – in other words, for walls. If water lies on them during freezing weather, the surfaces will flake very quickly. And they then look very unattractive indeed. For paving, use engineering bricks, which are very tough and will withstand any amount of frost.

Types of paving

Materials. Basically, there are three types of paving available – natural stone, reconstituted stone and concrete. Natural stone is generally considered to be the 'crème de la crème' of materials, especially if it is to be used around an

16

older property. It has two disadvantages. It is becoming very hard to come by, especially if you are looking for second-hand stone, but it is also extremely expensive. Often the cost lies in transport, so if you are lucky enough to live near a local source it may be a little cheaper. Most natural stone will cut easily with a chisel.

Reconstituted natural stone is an acceptable alternative. The only difference between this and concrete is that, instead of using flint ballast in the concrete, natural stone chippings and dust are used. This gives the stone a much 'softer' appearance, and makes it easier to cut by hand.

Concrete is so well known that it needs no description. It is generally cheaper than natural or reconstituted stone but it is difficult, if not impossible, to cut by hand. So the cost of hiring a stone saw must be taken into account. Some concrete slabs are coloured, and it should be remembered that the colours will almost certainly fade after a period of exposure to the elements.

Colour. Paving slabs are obtainable in a wide variety of colours, some of them initially quite vivid. Generally, highly coloured paving, unless perhaps you live in the south of France or in Bermuda, is difficult to live with. It is certainly not restful to the eye, and it is very difficult to select plants that will live happily with the bright colours. Perhaps the one exception is around the swimming pool.

Try to choose a colour that will match its surroundings. If, for example, you live in a stone cottage, it would be the height of folly to choose light grey, concrete slabs. They will always stand out like a sore thumb. In this case, if you can't afford the same natural stone, choose a colour and texture as near to the stone of the house as possible.

Naturally, brick walls in the garden are best chosen to match the walls of the house. If this is impossible, and the garden walls are to be built in close proximity to the house, it may be safer to choose a completely different brick, rather than finishing up with a 'near miss'.

Shape. Undoubtedly the most popular type of paving is rectangular. It can be bought in various sizes, so it is possible to make attractive 'random' patterns. For paving around a house, or in the garden, this is much to be desired. Square paving set in straight lines gives a much harder, 'municipal' effect, though it can be used to good effect where a strictly formal scheme is envisaged.

Hexagonal slabs tend, in my opinion, to look rather 'fussy', but are useful in large areas of rectangular paving to create a change in texture. It is also possible to buy 'fish-shaped' tiles, which slot together; these can look attractive in small areas but are time-consuming to lay.

Crazy paving is in a class of its own. The Victorians are to blame for the acres of crazy paving around even modern houses, where it is quite out of place. They have a lot to answer for. Crazy paving has a place in the garden of an old country cottage, but that's about all. It does *not* fit in with modern architecture at all. It has the one dubious advantage that it is possible to buy it very cheaply from the local authority yard. Here, damaged slabs that have been removed from pavements are stored, and they are often only too pleased to see the back of them. You may have to arrange your own transport though.

1. Undoubtedly, rectangular paving is the most popular choice for the do-it-yourselfer.

2. Crazy paving can look fine in the garden of an old house but can be out of place in newer gardens.

Surface finish. Slabs are available in a variety of finishes, from the very smooth, concrete pavings to those finished by exposing the aggregate to form a very rough surface.

Choice is very much a personal matter, but certain practical applications should be considered. Round the swimming pool, it is logical to choose the smoothest surface possible, for comfort when lying in the sun. As has already been mentioned, in shady areas where slabs are likely to become slippery, a non-slip surface is best.

Some pavings are made with a 'riven' finish to match the appearance of natural stone when it wears. Often these slabs can look very attractive and are an excellent alternative to natural stone.

It is also possible to buy pavings with a moulded surface made to represent another material entirely. Stable blocks can now be obtained in a slab, while others look very much like brick paving. These slabs tend to be quite expensive, but not nearly so costly as the real thing. Naturally, they are very much easier to lay.

3. Coloured paving tends to be a little garish, though it can be effective round a swimming pool.

Ordering

If you are laying slabs of one size, or if you use crazy paving, ordering is simple. Simply measure up the area, allow a couple of square metres for breakages, and order in square metres. But if you intend to use a random rectangular pattern, ordering is a little more complicated. There are two alternatives. You can draw out the area to scale and work out a pattern before you start. This way you can order just the number and sizes of slabs you need.

Altenatively you may prefer to work out the pattern as you lay the slabs, thus giving an entirely informal effect. In this case it will be impossible to work out in advance the exact number of each size you will need. The best method is to measure out the total area and divide it by the number of different sizes you intend to use. Then ask the merchant to deliver equal *areas* (not numbers) of each size. When you get near the end, you will be able to see more accurately what you need to finish the job. You should only need a few slabs, which can perhaps be picked up from the merchant by car, to avoid the additional cost of delivery.

3 Tools

Before starting on the work, make sure that you have all the tools you need. You will always discover that you have forgotten to buy the spirit level on a Sunday afternoon when the builder's merchant is closed. And more often than not, you will have just mixed a large batch of mortar that you won't be able to use. That's the Law of the Cussedness of Nature and should be guarded against.

Some tools you will be able to make yourself, but many will have to be bought. With a few exceptions, it is best to buy top-quality tools and to look after them. Many of them will be used in the garden or around the house later, so it will be money well spent.

Wheelbarrow

A good barrow will save a great deal of effort. There are many very pretty models on the market, but there is still nothing to beat the good, old-fashioned navvy-barrow. They are made for hard work and lots of it, and should last you a lifetime. Choose one with a pneumatic tyre. They are much easier to push when they are loaded, especially if the ground is rough.

Spade, fork and shovel

These basic gardening tools will be used time and time again in the garden. So again it is worth buying the best. If you can afford it buy a stainless-steel spade because they make the digging out a positive pleasure. For the fork and shovel ordinary forged steel is quite good enough. Don't be over-ambitious, especially with the shovel. Choose one you can comfortably work with all day.

Straightedge

It sounds obvious but it really is very important to make sure that your straightedge is straight. A lump of twisted softwood will be worse than useless, and your paving, walling or concrete will finish up all over the place.

Buy a piece of hardwood about 7.5cm × 2.5cm × 3m (3in × 1in × 10ft) and get the timber merchant to plane it straight on his planer. Then, just to make sure, hold it up to your eye, and sight down it. Any twists or deviations will easily be seen.

Trowels

For paving and walling, you will need two trowels. Again, buy the best. For handling mortar for both jobs, you'll need a large, bricklayer's trowel, and for pointing afterwards, a smaller pointing trowel is required.

Spirit level

Spirit levels are not cheap, so if you are unlikely to use them after the stonework job is completed, try to borrow from a friend, or even hire from a small tool agency. Ideally, you should have a small level, about 23cm(9in) long for working in restricted areas, and a 1m(3ft) level for general paving and walling work. If the worst comes to the worst, you can use the small level on top of the straightedge for levelling paving, but it is nothing like as convenient.

Club hammer

A 1.5kg(3lb) club hammer will be necessary for laying paving, and for cutting slabs and bricks. If you are doing a lot of paving, you'll ruin the handle, so an expensive hammer is a luxury.

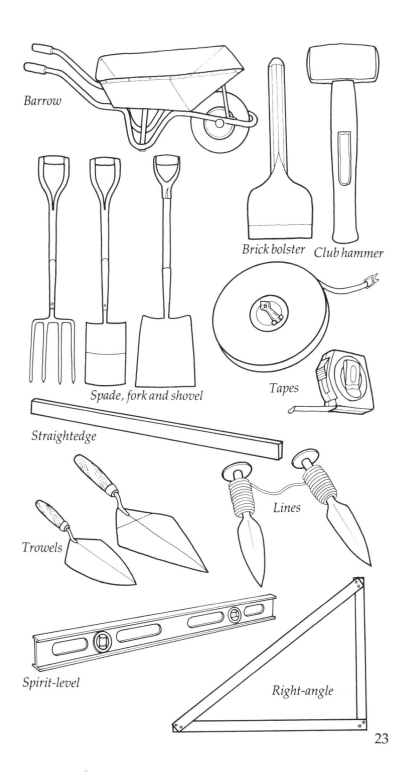

Barrow

Brick bolster Club hammer

Spade, fork and shovel

Tapes

Straightedge

Lines

Trowels

Spirit-level

Right-angle

23

You may, in fact, find that a hammer of this weight is a little clumsy to use. In this case, handle the hammer before buying and, if it feels too heavy, settle for a lighter one.

Bolsters

Ideally, you should buy a stone bolster and a brick bolster. But the heavier stone bolsters are rather difficult to obtain, so you may have to make do with a brick bolster for both jobs. With a little practice, it will do a perfectly good job of cutting stone. Again, since neither is likely to be used a lot after the stonework is done, you may prefer to borrow or hire.

Tapes

Measuring tapes are essential for many jobs in the new garden. It really is important to measure up accurately before committing your garden design to paper, and you'll need them again during the actual work. For measuring larger areas use a surveyor's tape, and for closer work you'll also need a good steel tape. Don't make do with your wife's dressmaking tape-measure or your son's school ruler. Slabs and bricks are made to accurate and uniform measurements so you will need to be accurate too.

Lines

For surveying, you will need a good garden line, and you will also find a bricklayer's line, which is thinner, invaluable. Make sure they are made of nylon, since this won't stretch. Brickies generally use special pins for holding their lines, but I have found a couple of large nails to be adequate.

Spot-board

When you are laying bricks, or pointing, you will find it much easier if the mortar is placed on a board. Builders call them 'spot-boards', but they are nothing more or less than a lump of wood about 1m × 1m(3ft × 3ft). You should be able to find a suitable piece knocking around behind the shed.

Right-angle

For surveying you will almost certainly need to measure a right-angle. For short measurements, use a carpenter's square, or preferably a roofing square. For measuring on a larger scale you can make a right-angle out of wood. Simply measure three lengths of scrap wood to form a 3,4,5 triangle, and nail them together. The angle between the two shortest sides will be a right-angle.

Bucket

You will certainly need a good, large, strong bucket for carrying water. Buy one of the strong, plastic variety from the builder's merchant. It will get plenty of use later.

Broom

One of the most useful tools of the trade, the broom should be in constant use. If you sweep up regularly, and keep the job clean at all times, the finished result will be much, much better. You'll need a stiff, yard broom for cleaning down the driveway after mixing concrete, and a soft broom for cleaning the slabs and brickwork.

Tools to hire

If you have a lot of concreting to do, you will find the hire of a small concrete mixer invaluable. It will save an enormous amount of time and effort and is well worth the expense.

For cutting concrete slabs, you can hire a stone saw, sometimes called an angle-grinder. This consists of a motorized abrasive wheel that will cut through almost anything. They are quite expensive to hire, and use up the discs at an alarming rate.

Maintenance

There is nothing worse than trying to work with tools that are encrusted with half a ton of hardened concrete. It is frustrating, time-consuming, and a sign of a bad workman. *Always* clean your tools in water at the end of every day's work, especially if you have borrowed or hired them. After washing them, dry them with a bit of old sacking and put them away where you'll find them straight away the following morning.

After work each day, make sure that your tools are well washed to remove all traces of cement.

4 Setting out

The importance of careful planning cannot be overstated. It really is vital to draw up a careful plan of the whole garden incorporating the patio, path or wall before starting on the job. Only in this way can the effect be visualized and the correct proportions ascertained.

Perhaps the most difficult task of the landscape gardener, even the professional, is to visualize the finished effect of any feature in the garden. The task is made very much easier if the proposed feature is first committed to paper. After that, it is well worthwhile marking out the site with pegs and string to assist the imagination.

To make drawings that are accurate enough for the purpose does not require sophisticated instruments, nor do you need to take a course in surveying. With the possible exception of a good surveyor's tape, you will almost certainly find all you need in the garage or the garden shed. A very basic understanding of simple geometry completes the necessary equipment.

Measuring up

The first essential is to measure up and draw the boundaries of the garden. If the site is exactly rectangular, this is a very simple matter. But, in my experience, gardens rarely are.

So you must start by finding two objects that are fixed. The easiest way is to use the two corners of the house.

Equip yourself with a clip-board, (a piece of scrap plywood and a bulldog clip), and a piece of paper. Start by drawing roughly the shape of the garden, with the house in the drawing. There is no need to be at all accurate at this stage.

Now, from each corner of the house, measure to the corners of the garden and mark the measurements on the drawing. Then measure any fixed objects, such as trees, or perhaps the clothes post or the coal bunker if you don't intend to move them, in exactly the same way. Always make two measurements from each corner of the house.

In order to be able to check your measurements later, it is as well also to measure the lengths of the boundaries. With all these measurements drawn into the rough drawings, you are now ready to start on the accurate plan.

On a large piece of paper (squared paper makes the job much easier) draw in the house. It must be drawn to scale, and this is normally something like 5cm to 1m or, if you prefer to work in feet and inches, about 2in to 1yd.

Now, using a pair of compasses, draw an arc from one corner of the house to the first corner of the garden as measured on your rough plan. Repeat this exercise from the other corner, so that the two arcs cross. Where they cross is the corner of the garden.

Repeat this for the second corner, and draw a line joining the two. Confirm now that your measurements are correct by working out the distance between the two corners and checking the measurement you made on the rough plan. Do the same to establish all the points you measured and you have an accurate, scale drawing of the garden.

Make this drawing your 'master-plan'. Ink it in if you feel like making a really professional job of it, because you will no doubt need it for some time, especially if you are embarking on a new garden.

Fix the master-plan to a board and pin a piece of tracing paper over it. Then, all your drawing can be done on the tracing paper without defacing the master. You will probably want to do a lot of scribbling on the paper before you arrive at a scheme that fully satisfies you and you may want to scrap several pieces of tracing paper in the process.

If you are working on a new garden, the best bet is to

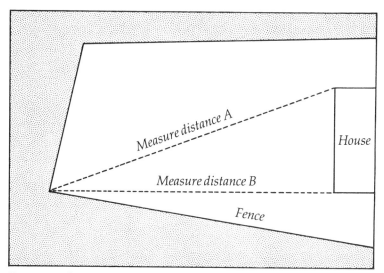

Fig. 1. To 'fix' any point on your plan, accurately measure from both corners of the house.

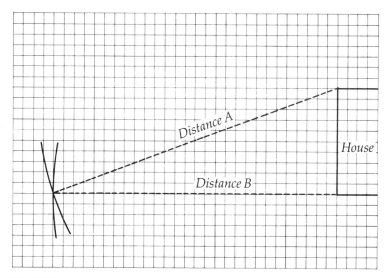

Fig 2. Now draw two arcs on squared paper to a predetermined scale. The point is fixed where they cross.

plan the whole scheme right from the start, even if you don't intend to do all the work immediately. Draw in your lawn, the patio, paths, walling and borders and any other features you intend to build. Fiddle around with the drawing until you are absolutely satisfied that the plan is exactly as you want it. It is much better to make mistakes at this stage than later.

Marking out

If you have drawn your plan on squared paper, transferring the plan to the site is a fairly simple matter. Start from one of your fixed points – again, the house is the easiest – measure up, and bang in a peg at, say, the corner of the patio. You may need to measure right-angles during the process of setting out, and this is where your 3,4,5 triangle will come in useful. Then, always working from the drawing, set out pegs at the remaining corners.

Now, join the pegs with string to show exactly the outline of the proposed feature. Then, take a walk around it looking from all angles. If it helps, go up and view it from the bedroom window, or from the sitting room if that is where you will see it when you're in the house. If it doesn't look right – change it. There is a golden rule in landscape design that 'if it *looks* right, it *is* right'. Because a plan looks good on paper, it doesn't necessarily follow that it will also look right when viewed from another angle, so that it doesn't offend the eye.

If your feature incorporates curves, the drawing and setting out process is a little more complicated. Start by drawing, either freehand, or with compasses or a drawing instrument known as a 'French curve'. When it comes to transferring this curve to the land, you must make a series of measurements from a fixed line (perhaps the boundary fence or the house) at intervals. Mark out these measurements with a peg, join them with string, and you have your curve.

Circles, of course, are easy, but make sure when you do the drawing, that you are able to locate exactly the centre

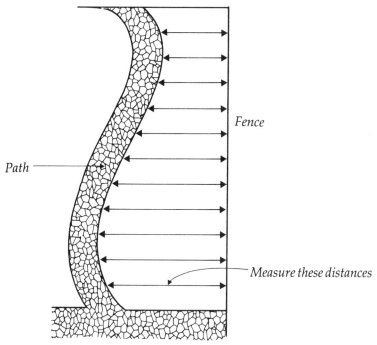

Fence

Path

Measure these distances

Fig 3. To mark out a curve on the ground, measure at fixed
intervals from a straight boundary.

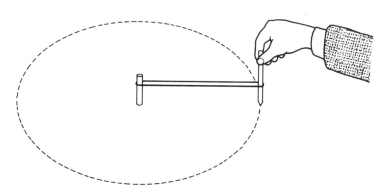

Fig 4. To mark out a circle, bang a peg into the centre and use a
loop of string.

of the circle. It's then an easy matter to bang in a peg, measure the radius of the circle from the plan, and mark it out with a piece of string and a sharpened stake.

With curves, even more than with straight lines, you may feel that you want to change the shape a little once you see it on the ground. Don't let that worry you at all. Remember, 'if it looks right, it *is* right'.

5 Preparation

If the site for your patio, path or walling is infested with weeds, it may well be worth while getting rid of them once and for all. Strong-growing perennial weeds can often push up paving and even crack concrete. If there is a vigorous tree nearby, such a as a poplar, sycamore or willow, then the roots will almost certainly cause you trouble.

If the weeds are only annuals, there is no point in wasting money on weedkillers. You will, in most cases, have a certain amount of excavation to do before you start on the stonework, and this will rid the site.

Invasive perennial weeds, such as couch grass, convolvulus, nettles, etc., should certainly be killed before any soil is excavated. Apart from the damage that any remaining roots would cause, there is no point in transferring the weeds from one part of the garden to another. This is only laying up trouble for the future.

I am a great believer in using a weedkiller that will not taint the soil and prevent anything growing for a long period. Certainly, it would be possible to use something cheap like sodium chlorate, but this does have its disadvantages. Firstly, it will make the soil unsuitable for growing for at least six months and possibly longer. This means that it cannot be carted to another part of the garden and used to make up a border or to level a new lawn area. It has the further disadvantage that it will 'creep' in the soil. If, for example, you are treating an area close to a border, even if you are careful not to allow the weedkiller to touch the cultivated soil, it will spread and damage plants.

If you wish to grow plants in the paved area, the roots

may well, at a later stage, reach down into the infected soil, and this will kill them. It is always worth spending a little more to avoid these hazards.

For perennial weeds, the material to use is called *glyphosate*. It is sold at present by Murphy Chemicals under the brand name 'Tumbleweed'. It can be applied with a watering can, but it is much better sprayed on with an ordinary garden sprayer. Not only does this save quite a bit of money because it puts less of the weedkiller on, but strangely enough, it is also more effective. The weedkiller is taken in by the leaves and translocated to the roots. Here it prevents them from storing or manufacturing food, so the plant dies. Naturally, it takes quite a time to show the effects, and you must leave at least a week for the weeds to absorb the herbicide, before starting to excavate. But then, you'll have a really clean site, and no worries for the future.

Trees are more of a problem. If they are vigorous and surface rooting like those already mentioned, the only answer is to pull them out. Bear in mind that they may also damage the foundations of the house if they are too close, in which case no time should be lost in removing them. If you do, make sure you plant at least one more tree in another part of your garden. Deeper rooting or less vigorous trees will cause no problems, and should be left in.

Excavating and levelling for paving

If you are laying even a small area of paving, it is important to find the correct levels and to allow for sufficient fall to take water away. After all, the paved area is often used specifically because grass can become too wet, so you won't want puddles.

If you are laying your patio next to the house, then correct levelling is of paramount importance. All modern houses, and many old ones too, have a damp-proof course (DPC) set in the brickwork just above ground level. This is there to prevent water from entering the bricks and rising up by capillary action. Without it, the water would even-

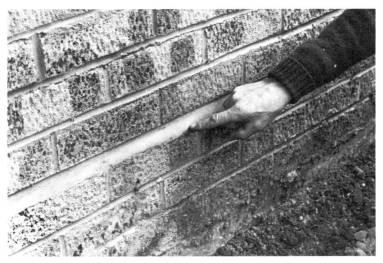

1. The damp-proof course can be easily recognized by the thicker layer of mortar between the bricks.

tually seep into the wall and reappear inside the house, with disastrous results.

It is quite easy to recognize the course of bricks in which the DPC has been embedded. The joint of mortar will be about twice the thickness of the other joints. On older houses, it was often the practice to use a layer of slates, or even a course of hard, blue engineering bricks, and of course, these can easily be seen.

Make sure that the finished level of the paving is at least two courses of bricks below the DPC. This will ensure that, even in heavy rain, no water splashes up above it.

If, as is sometimes the case with new houses, the builders have already laid a strip of concrete that finishes just two courses below the DPC, then I'm afraid there is no alternative but to dig it up again. Don't skimp by laying the paving on top of the concrete, or you may find yourself replastering the sitting room wall!

The first job is to mark out your patio area accurately allowing about 7.5cm(3in) extra all round. This will allow a small margin of error. Then, dig out the soil to a very rough level, carting the soil off the site.

Now you'll need a number of wooden pegs. These can be made out of rough, scrap wood, but should be fairly stout. Make them about 30–45cm(12–18in) long, and if you expect to take some time over the job it is worth giving them a coat of white paint. They will be there for the duration of the job and believe me, they are the easiest things in the world to trip over, so it's worth making them clearly visible.

Before banging in the pegs, mark a line on them to indicate the finished level of the concrete base. The position of the mark is easily worked out. Starting from the top of the peg, allow the thickness of the paving, plus an extra 2.5cm(1in) for the mortar bed. Thus, if the paving is 3.75cm(1½in) thick, the line should be marked 5.2cm(2½in) from the top of the peg. For 5cm(2in) thick paving, mark the line 7.5cm(3in) from the top.

Start by banging in the first peg near to the wall. Using the spirit level, make sure that it is at least two courses below the DPC. Now, using the straightedge and spirit level, bang in a line of pegs along the wall at exactly the same level.

2. Mark a line on the wooden pegs to allow for the thickness of the paving plus the depth of the mortar.

3. Start by banging the first peg in close to the wall, and make sure it is well below the damp-proof course.

4. Now the second row of pegs can be set, ensuring that there is a gentle fall away from the house.

The second row of pegs is set a distance away from the wall in line with the first row to form a right-angle with the house wall. Bear in mind when setting this row, that a slight fall will be needed.

The fall need not be great, and generally about 2.5cm(1in) in 3m(10ft) is sufficient. If your second row of pegs is 1.5m(5ft) from the first row, then they should be set about 13mm(½in) lower. To do this, simply cut a small scrap of wood 13mm(½in) thick, and place it on the top of the peg to be set. Then with your straightedge running from the peg nearest the house to the one you are levelling, tap down the peg until the spirit level shows it exactly level. Remove the piece of 13mm(½in) wood, and the peg will be at the correct level. The remainder of the row can be set from this peg. It is a good idea to check the odd peg here and there with those in the first row, using your scrap of wood. At this stage, you can't be too careful.

When all the pegs are in, make sure that you warn the other members of your family that they are there. Tripping over one peg and landing on another can cause a nasty injury and worse, it may upset your levels!

Having set all the pegs, you can now accurately dig out to the correct levels for concrete. If you are making a patio that will only be used for pedestrian traffic, and the soil is well consolidated, you will need a concrete base no more than 7.5cm(3in) thick. If the soil has been deeply cultivated, or contains a high proportion of organic matter, 10cm(4in) is better. Bear in mind, also, that builder's excavations will always settle, however well they are beaten down afterwards. This is especially so round new houses where the footings have been dug out by machine and refilled later.

In this case it may be better to dig out deeply and refill with about 30cm(1ft) of well-consolidated hardcore covered by 15cm(6in) of concrete. This is also necessary if you are building a driveway that will have to take vehicles.

Work out the necessary depth of concrete or hardcore and concrete and dig out to leave that thickness below the line marked on the pegs. When digging out, try not to dig too deeply so that you have to refill later. If you do make a mistake, refill with hardcore and tamp it down well. If you refill with soil, it will always settle a little, leaving spaces beneath the concrete base.

The soil you dig out can generally be used somewhere else in the garden, but there may be times when it is better to cart it away. Many builders dig out the footings for the

5. When digging out around the pegs, try not to dig too deeply so that the soil has to be refilled.

house and simply leave the subsoil on top of the existing topsoil. This is always best carted away, since it is worse than useless spread on top of the garden soil.

Because you may wish to use the soil on another part of the garden, it can be seen that if you are embarking on a new garden it is best to do all the 'hard' landscaping first.

Levelling for walls

The preparation for walling is much the same, except that the depth of concrete for the footing will vary according to the height of the wall. For a wall under 1m(3ft) high, the concrete need only be about 10cm(4in) thick, but for higher walls, you should allow at least 15cm(6in).

The width of the footing is also important. It must be at least twice the width of the proposed wall. So, if you are building a single brick wall, make the footing at least 23cm(9in) wide. For a double brick wall, it should be 45cm(18in) wide. The top of the pegs in this case, are used to show the finished level of the concrete footing, and they should finish a couple of inches below soil level, so that no concrete shows.

Bear in mind also that walling is always built level. The footing should never slope. If the ground slopes, it will be necessary to 'step' the footings, and the steps should be in multiples of the thickness of your brick or stone.

6. Footings for walls must be dug out deeper and should be at least twice the width of the wall.

6 Drainage

A large expanse of paving will trap a great deal of water. Very often, the patio at the back of the house will be as big as one side of the house roof, and will collect as much rainwater. It is important to allow for this to get away.

Firstly, though it has been said before in previous chapters, it *must* be remembered that the paving should slope away from the house. The slope need not be great enough to be noticeable, but it should be sufficient to ensure that, even in a flash storm, the water has no chance to build up against the wall of the house.

Very often, provided this is borne in mind, drainage is no problem. If, for example, the paving slopes away to a flower border, the water will simply run off the surface and into the flower bed. In wet areas, you may have to bear this

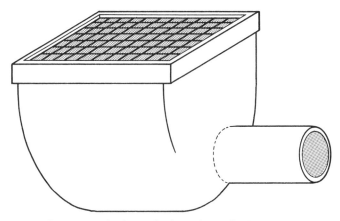

Fig 1. A gulley trap which can be bought at the builder's merchants. Set it in the patio.

in mind when planting the border, since it will generally be wetter than other parts of the garden.

If the patio slopes down to grass, there is a chance that water may be trapped. When building the patio, it should be made at such a level that the grass is very slightly proud of the paving. This will enable the mower to cut right to the edge without difficulty, and the edges will be no problem to cut. The grass will, however, form a natural barrier to escaping water.

If this is the case, dig out a trench about 15cm(6in) deep and 30cm(1ft) wide at the edge of the paving before levelling the soil for the lawn.

The trench should be filled with a suitable drainage material, such as crushed clinker or gravel, before covering with about 7.5cm(3in) of soil. This sort of depth will be quite enough for the grass, and will provide an adequate drain for excess water. If the soil is very heavy and natural drainage poor, the width and depth of the drain can be increased.

So far, so good. But the problems really start to arise when the garden slopes up away from the house. In this case, it may be necessary to build a retaining wall at the far end of the patio. It can be clearly seen that this creates a

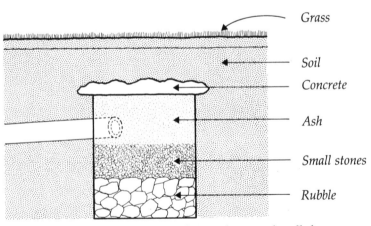

Grass

Soil

Concrete

Ash

Small stones

Rubble

Fig 2. Dig a large soakaway in the garden to take all the excess water from the patio.

42

well that, if no provision were made, would turn into an impromptu swimming pool at every shower of rain. In this case it is necessary to make special provision to take the water away. Thought must be given to this at a very early stage in the building of the patio, since drainage must be one of the first jobs.

On most patios, only one drain will be necessary, but if the area of paving is very large, it may warrant two. Start by selecting a point somewhere near the middle of the patio at the end furthest from the house, for the gulley that will collect the excess water. When setting your level pegs, you must ensure that they slope not only away from the house, but also from either end towards the centre, where the gulley will be set.

The water is collected by means of a glazed earthenware gulley trap. They are easily obtainable at any good builder's merchant. From the outlet of the gulley trap, set a number of earthenware drainage pipes to a soakaway in the garden.

The soakaway can be either under the lawn or in a flower border. Bear in mind that, if it is sited in the border, you will probably need to sink it lower to allow for a sufficient depth of soil to accommodate plants. Under the lawn, a covering of about 15cm(6in) of soil will be enough.

The soakaway is built by digging a large pit. Naturally, the larger the patio, the larger the pit should be. The hole is filled with rubble at the bottom, covered by a depth of gravel with a covering of concrete over the top to prevent soil filtering down and blocking the drain.

If you are building a retaining wall, bear in mind also that the water will be pushing against the back of the wall too. Unless provision is made for it to escape, the water could build up to such an extent in a wet season, that the pressure could push the wall over. To avoid this, build in 'weep holes' in the brick or stonework, to allow the water to escape. The simplest way to do this is to leave a space in the second row of bricks at about 1m(1yd) intervals. However, the finished effect will be much more attractive if earthenware drainage pipes are set in the spaces.

Avoid the temptation to plant these all-important 'safety-valves' since roots of plants can mass together to choke the hole and block the escaping water.

However, on high walls that are built to retain soil on the other side, it is a good idea to leave a few more holes at intervals higher up the wall, specifically for plants. Though the roots will prevent some water escaping, their combined effect will certainly contribute something to the drainage, and they will look attractive into the bargain.

One final point on drainage that should be borne in mind at the planning stage. If you intend to lay an area of uneven surface, like cobbles or stable blocks, remember that it is much more difficult to provide adequate drainage. They should therefore not be laid in areas where it is important to maintain a dry surface.

7 Concreting

A knowledge of concrete and concreting is essential for all 'hard' landscaping work. If you are laying the base for a paved patio the finish need only be rough, but the principles are much the same. If you are concreting a driveway or a path the finish must be good and the work thorough if a really strong result is to be obtained.

Shuttering

A base for paving requires no shuttering to keep the concrete within bounds and to form a neat, finished edge. But for a driveway, where the edge of the concrete will be seen, it is essential.

Generally, for domestic jobs, the shuttering can be made out of wood. It is possible to hire metal 'formers' but these can be expensive and the depth of concrete required is not usually enough to warrant them. Normally, 10cm × 2.5cm(4in × 1in) sawn timber will be adequate for paths. For driveways, where a greater depth of concrete is required, use 15cm × 2.5cm (6in × 1in).

The shuttering is nailed to pegs driven into the ground at about 1m(3ft) intervals. Make sure that the shuttering is nailed to the *inside* of the pegs, so that they are not concreted in. This way, the finish of the edge is neater, and the shuttering can be removed afterwards. If the path or driveway is to be curved, the timber can easily be bent by making a series of saw-cuts on the inside of the curve.

When you are setting the shuttering, make sure that it is level from side to side, and that the slope (if there is one) is even.

For a driveway that is to take vehicles, you will need to set a layer of hardcore underneath the concrete, so dig out for this inside the shuttering after you have set it. Generally, 15cm(6in) of hardcore, well compacted, will be sufficient. Hardcore can consist of builders rubble, generally obtainable from demolition sites, or of crushed stone from the quarry.

Concrete

Once the shuttering is in position, and the hardcore down, the concrete can be ordered. Before doing so, make sure that you have the necessary tools for the job to hand. For a driveway, it is advisable to use a vibrating board. This consists of a long board with a handle on each end. Set on top of the board is an engine that serves to vibrate it as you move it along. This useful piece of equipment can be hired from most small tool hirers, and will make the job easier, stronger and very well finished. You will also need a shovel and the help of a friend or neighbour.

1. The easiest way to buy concrete is readi-mix, but you will have to be well organized.

46

The easiest way to buy concrete is ready-mixed. This saves a lot of back-breaking work, but it has two disadvantages. Firstly it is more expensive than mixing your own, but perhaps more importantly, you need to be well organized before it arrives. Don't, for example, do as a friend of mine did. He realized only when he had a 10-tonne load of wet concrete in the middle of his driveway that he had left his car in the garage! He was without the use of it for several days.

Make sure that everything is ready, and you'll save yourself a lot of work. One other advantage with ready-mix, is that the merchant will know exactly what sort of mix you require for your particular job, so you'll cut out one of the biggest causes of mistakes.

If you decide to mix your own, it is well worth hiring a small mixer if you have any amount to do. Not only is the work reduced to an acceptable minimum, but it will make a better job of the mixing too. For small areas, of course, the mixing can be done by hand.

Concrete for paths, driveways and the base for a patio is made up with sharp sand, aggregate (gravel) and cement. It is easiest to buy the sand and aggregate already mixed, and most merchants will be able to supply it. To decide how much you need, start by measuring the area to be covered. This is then multiplied by the depth of concrete required to give the volume required. Most builder's merchants will be able to translate this into tonnes of aggregate (discount the volume of cement, which makes little or no difference). As an example, 1 tonne(1ton) of aggregate will give 12sq.m(12sq.yds) of concrete 7.5cm(3in) thick. If the concrete is to be 15cm(6in) thick, it will naturally cover half this area. For each tonne of aggregate, you will need eight bags of cement.

For a driveway or for the base of paving or walling, the concrete should be made by mixing eight parts by volume of aggregate with one part of Portland cement.

When mixing concrete, remember that the drier the mix is, the stronger will be the concrete when it sets. So, you should make the mix as dry as possible, consistent with it being workable. For a smooth finish, it will have to be much wetter than that used for the base for paving. Where this sort of rough finish is all that is necessary, the concrete can in fact be put down dry. Moisture from the soil beneath will eventually ensure that the concrete sets hard. ·

2. If you have a large amount to mix, it is well worthwhile hiring a small concrete mixer.

3. To hand-mix concrete, start by adding the cement to the aggregate and turning it thoroughly.

4. Make a hole in the middle of the heap and add water. Remember to make it as dry as you can work with.

5. Now push some of the outside of the heap of aggregate into the middle of the hole.

6. Finish mixing by thoroughly turning the heap again, making sure all the mixture is evenly wet.

7. To make a path, start by setting the shuttering, levelling across with a straightedge and spirit level.

8. Fill inside the shuttering with concrete and tamp down with a piece of timber. Finish with a 'sawing' action.

9. At the end of the day, cover what you have done with sacking and block the end with wood, giving a clean start the next day.

52

10. If you wish to make a textured finish, simply mark lines in the hardening cement with a broom.

11. For a smooth finish, the surface should be stroked gently with a metal plasterer's float.

12. Concrete for a paving base need not be well finished. Barrow it onto the site, avoiding the pegs.

13. Spread the concrete around, making sure that it comes no higher than the mark on the pegs.

14. For this sort of base, it is sufficient so consolidate the concrete by treading it down.

For a driveway or a path that is not to be paved afterwards, the mix should be wetter. The concrete is then poured into the shuttered area, and the board worked backwards and forwards across the top of the shuttering until the 'fat' rises to the top to form a good surface. This way, the finished surface of the concrete will be slightly ribbed, and it is worth leaving it like this to make a non-slip surface. If you require a smooth surface, you will have to go over it with a plasterer's float afterwards.

Once the concrete is down, it must be 'cured'. This is done by covering the surface with wet sacking or hessian, to ensure that it dries slowly. It will be much stronger this way. Curing is unnecessary when laying the base for paving. All you need do is to rake out the dry concrete so that it comes up to the line previously marked on the pegs, and consolidate it by treading. Make sure that the base never comes over the marked line, or you may not be able to knock the paving slabs down low enough to level them.

When concreting for the foundations of walling, the

trench itself should retain the concrete, so there is no need for shuttering. Bring the concrete up to the top of the pegs, and tamp it down well with a baulk of timber. Though a really fine finish is unnecessary, the top should be reasonably smooth and level.

If you are concreting in the winter when there is a danger of frost, make sure that you can cover the whole area at night, or mix a proprietary concrete anti-freeze in with the mixing water.

8 Rectangular paving

There is no doubt that for the do-it-yourselfer, artificial rectangular paving slabs are the favourite method of making a path or patio. They are reasonably inexpensive, they look good, and they are certainly the easiest to lay.

The first job is to decide on the pattern of laying them. It is a fairly simple matter to work out a pattern on paper first, in which case, as has already been suggested, it will be easier to order just the quantity you require. Alternatively, they can be laid in an entirely random fashion, working out the pattern as you go along. To work this way you will have to think three or four slabs ahead in order to avoid long 'tramlines', but once you get the hang of it, it is not difficult.

The mortar

Slabs are laid on a mortar made with three parts of soft builders sand to one of Portland cement. When mixing, it is important not to make the mix too wet. If it is, the mortar will 'slump' when the slabs are rested on it, and they will be difficult, if not impossible, to level. Again, if the weather is likely to be frosty, mix a little anti-freeze in with the water.

Before starting, get yourself a 'spot-board'. This is simply a piece of timber large enough to take a fair pile of mortar. It will save you a lot of waste mortar. Never try to scoop the mortar out of a bucket. That way it's difficult and very frustrating. It's also a good idea to put a few slabs of different sizes to hand. This will save a lot of walking about once you get started.

Laying the slabs

The first slab is definitely the most important, since this sets the pattern of level and line for all the rest. It is well worth taking a lot of trouble over this one. Get it right and you'll have no problems with the rest.

Start by placing five mounds of mortar on the base where the slab is to lay. They should be at each corner with one, slightly smaller mound in the centre.

Lift the slab and place it on the mounds. Never try to lower it on while one side of the slab is resting on the ground. This way you will flatten two of the mounds of mortar, and levelling will be difficult.

When the slab is resting on the mortar, check that it is aligned correctly. This is most important, especially if the slabs are adjacent to the house wall. If the first slab of a long patio or path is just the slightest bit out of line, by the time you reach the other end it will be several inches out. To allow for a small margin of error, set the first slab about 2.5cm(1in) away from the wall.

Then set up a line so that it runs along the top edge of the slab, nearest to the wall. Take the line to the other end and fix it so that it, too, is 2.5cm(1in) from the wall. Now it is an easy matter to ensure that the top of the slab is exactly in line with the line.

Now the slab must be levelled. Place the straightedge on top at one end, and on the nearest peg at the other. Tap it down with the handle of the club hammer until the straightedge lies exactly flat along the top of the slab. Always use the *handle* of a hammer for tapping down the slabs since the metal head is very likely to crack it. You will probably find, at the end of the job, that you need a new handle, but that is a small price to pay if all the slabs are intact.

If the slab is meant to be level one way, it is worth checking it with the spirit level at this stage. It will, of course, slope away from the house, so the level will not register true that way.

The second and subsequent slabs are laid in exactly the

1. Mix the mortar and set out five small heaps where the first slab is to be laid.

2. The slab is now rested on top of the heaps of mortar a little way away from the wall.

3. Tap the slab down carefully until it is exactly level with the nearest peg.

4. Now, using the straightedge, make sure it is also level the other way.

5. It is important to ensure that the first slab is exactly in line with the wall.

6. With the first slab correctly positioned, the remaining slabs can now be laid.

same way, butting them up tight with the last slab laid. Generally, if you are using artificial slabs, there is no need to leave a space for pointing. Indeed, the crack between the slabs will serve to take any surface water away quickly. If you are laying natural stone paving, you may find that the edges are not even enough to allow close butting. In this case, leave a gap of about 13mm(½in) and point it in with mortar afterwards.

If you are working to a pattern, keep the plan handy, and it is a simple matter to select the next slab you need by referring to the plan. If you are working out the pattern as you go along, you will need to think ahead. It is important to avoid long, straight lines, so as soon as you see a line becoming unacceptably long, 'break' it by placing the next slab across it.

As the paving proceeds, check regularly with the straightedge that the slabs are level with the pegs. There is no need, of course, to check for alignment after the first slab is laid, since this decides the line for all the others.

As you come to a peg and it is in the way, either break it off, or drive it down into the concrete base.

When you have set each slab, try to 'rock' it on its heaps of mortar. Inevitably, some slabs will rock, and the only thing to do then is to take them up and lay them again.

Cutting slabs

Inevitably, there will be obstructions in the paving, like a gulley surround or an inspection cover, and this may well mean that slabs will have to be cut. If you are using straight concrete slabs, you will, I'm afraid, find them very difficult to cut with a hammer and chisel. In this case, it is best to hire a special stone saw. These consist of a motorized cutting disc, and they will cut through concrete quite easily.

Slabs made with stone chipping aggregate can be cut with a hammer and a brick bolster. Cutting them in half is surprisingly easy, but if you have to cut out an intricate shape, be prepared to break a few at first.

7. As the pegs get in the way of the next slab, tap them down or knock them out.

8. It is a good practice to keep the broom in use continually to prevent mortar stains.

9. At the end of the days work, clean up the mortar at the edge of each slab.

10. The final job is to point in between the slabs and the wall with dryish mortar.

Start by measuring up the slab and marking the line of the cut on the face (upper) side. Tip the slab on its side and cut a nick in each edge. Using the nick as a guide, mark the line of the cut on the reverse side of the slab.

Now lean the slab up against your leg and cut down the mark carefully with the hammer and brick bolster. Tap fairly gently, to cut a slight nick in the slab. Turn the slab round, and repeat the operation on the reverse side. Then turn it round again and cut the front line again, repeating the process until the slab falls in half. It really is not as difficult as it sounds. The secret lies in knowing just how hard to tap, and in having the patience to do the job gradually and slowly. Unless you are a very handy handyman (or woman), you can be sure that you will break the odd slab or two before you finally get the knack of cutting, so make sure you allow for a few breakages in your initial order.

If you find that cutting is impossible, or if you are working with concrete slabs, the alternative is to fill the awkward spaces with cement when the paving is completed. You can buy cement colouring powders, so that the concrete can be matched in colour to the slabs, making a fairly unobtrusive job.

As you progress with the paving, keep a soft broom handy. This is one of the more important tools in your kit and its use should not be neglected. If you drop a bit of mortar on the surface of the slabs, wait until it dries, but sweep it off before it hardens.

If you cannot finish the whole job in one day, make sure that, before you pack up for the night, you cut away any excess mortar that might be squeezing out from underneath the slabs. If you allow it to harden, you will have to chisel it away before you can lay the next slab

Pointing

If you have laid the paving with spaces between the slabs, they will have to be pointed in. This is done with a slightly stronger mortar, mixing two parts of sand to one of cement. The mortar can be worked in between the slabs

11. To cut paving, mark a line on the face of the slab and then cut a groove in each edge.

12. Leaning the slab against your leg, gently tap with the club hammer and brick bolster, both sides of the slab.

with a trowel and smoothed over. This is quite a time-consuming job, however. A quicker way is to brush the dry mix into the spaces. Make sure that the slabs are perfectly dry when you do this or the mortar will stain them. When all the spaces are filled, cover the entire area with about 13mm(½in) of soft sand, and lightly water it. Later the sand can be brushed off again, and the job's done.

Once the paving is down, it is vital that it should not be trodden on for several days. Make sure that you warn your family and friends and, to make doubly sure, put a few obstructions in the way to remind them. The wheelbarrow with the straightedge leaning against it is generally sufficient.

Finally, when you have finished each evening, and even before you take time to stand back and admire your handiwork, make sure that you wash all your tools thoroughly. Believe me, nothing is worse than trying to work with tools that are caked in cement, or humping a barrow with half a hundredweight of hard cement stuck to it. Don't forget, particularly, to wash the barrow wheel. This is often forgotten and only makes for a hard life.

9 Paving on sand

Who hasn't seen local authority paviors laying pavement slabs on sand? Certainly this is common practice and pavements rarely have to be replaced. This has led to the common belief that laying slabs on sand is perfectly adequate in all circumstances. Not true. In fact, it is fraught with dangers.

Firstly, the men you have watched laying slabs in the streets are experts. It really is not at all easy to level slabs that are set in sand. This necessitates getting just the right thickness of sand underneath the slab so that, when it is tapped down, it is exactly level with its neighbours and will not sink further. That sort of judgement takes a lot of experience.

But the main disadvantage with laying on sand is that the ground beneath it invariably sinks. Pavements are often laid either on soil that has been compacted by millions of pairs of feet over the years, or on a deep layer of hardcore that has been rolled with a really heavy road roller to compact it solid. Not easy in your back garden. This is particularly so when paving is being laid next to a new house. Invariably, the footings for the building are taken out with a mechanical digger. This digs a trench much too wide, and is refilled afterwards. However much the soil is then compacted, it will *always* sink a little, and the paving will end up at all different levels. This makes it dangerous and unsightly. So, unless the soil underneath the paving has been well compacted over a period of years, or you can provide a deep, well-consolidated layer of hardcore, play safe and lay the slabs on concrete as described in the previous chapter.

Provided all these conditions are fulfilled, then laying on sand is feasible. Use sharp sand, and mix a little dry Portland cement in with it at the ratio of about six to one. This will 'stabilize' the sand and help prevent it sinking.

Set the first slab as described previously but, instead of placing it on five points of mortar, make the sand bed level underneath the whole slab. The depth of the bed should be such that the slab has to be tapped down well to get it level. Because more tapping down is needed, it is unwise to use slabs less than 5cm(2in) thick, as many breakages are bound to occur. Ideally, go for 5cm(2in) slabs that have been made on a press as opposed to in a mould.

Align the slab to the wall, and check for level against the nearest peg, exactly as described for laying on mortar. With the first slab down, it will be a little easier to judge the amount of sand needed for the next one to allow for full compaction. But it must be stressed that this is the most difficult part of the job, and you must be prepared to take up a few and re-lay them if they are not level or compacted enough.

Slabs laid on sand *must* be pointed in between. This means that a space must be left between each slab to allow for the concrete fillet. To make sure that the space is exactly the same each time, it's a good idea to cut some pieces of wood about 13mm(½in) thick to place between each slab to guage the space accurately. The pointing in is important to add strength, and to prevent water washing through between the slabs and washing the sand out. For the same reason, it is necessary to cement a fillet right round the edge of the paving to prevent the sand washing out from underneath.

The mortar for the pointing is made with two parts by volume of soft builders sand, to one part Portland cement. It can be put in wet with a trowel, or brushed in dry, though naturally, that used for the fillet round the edge must be trowelled in.

When mixing the mortar for pointing, unless the whole lot can be done in one go, it is wise to mix it accurately by measuring it out with a bucket. If it is simply roughly measured by the shovel-full, the quantities will vary with each mix, and the colour of the resulting pointing will also vary.

Finally, remember when laying slabs on sand, that the paving will be suitable for pedestrian traffic only. Never, never run the car over them, or they will almost certainly move and will probably crack.

10 Stepping stones

Sometimes, it is necessary to make a path in the lawn. It may be to run alongside the washing-line, or it may be for access across the garden. It may even be desirable to do so for purely aesthetic reasons. Well done, paths can look attractive.

If your land is on the heavy side, it is quite likely that the soil will lay wet. Constant traffic, especially in the winter, will soon make bare patches in the grass, and these will quickly be colonized by weeds and moss. In this case, some sort of hard path is essential.

1. Lay out the stepping stones first and walk across them to ensure they are in the right place.

2. Cut round the slab with a spade or edging tool, and lift out the turf.

But it is often a mistake, especially in a small garden, to cut the lawn up into strips with a solid path. This has the visual effect of making the garden appear smaller and is rarely easy on the eye. One way round this problem is to lay stepping stones with grass strips in between to give the feeling of continuity across the lawn.

Stepping-stone paths can be straight or curved, depending on the design of the garden. But above all, they should be comfortable to walk on. There is nothing more annoying than to walk down a stepping-stone path that is so designed that, even if you start out with your feet on the first slab, you finish up walking on the grass in between.

To get over this, start by laying the slabs on the grass and actually walking on them. This exercise will also give you the opportunity to look carefully at the path, and to move the slabs about until the most pleasing effect is obtained.

With the slabs laid in position, it is an easy matter to cut round them with a sharp spade or a half-moon edging tool.

3. Place a little sand in the bottom of the hole to enable you to level the slab easily.

Then lift the slab, and remove the turf underneath it. Try to take the turf with just enough soil to enable you to lay about 2.5cm(1in) of sand and leave the stone a little below the grass level. Bear in mind that the lawn will have to be cut, and that the mower will need to ride over the top of the slabs. Otherwise, you will be letting yourself in for a lot of extra work.

Mix the sand with a little cement, and tap the slab down onto the bed so that it is level. Eventually, the edges of the grass will break down a little, and you may need to trim them back from time to time with the edging tool.

4. Tap the slab down so that the surface is just a little below the level of the grass.

11 Crazy paving

Think carefully before you decide to lay crazy paving. It is certainly cheaper than rectangular paving, especially if you buy it from the local council yard. But it will only give a pleasing effect in certain situations. Generally it can be said that it just doesn't fit in with modern architecture. Somehow it looks too fussy and old fashioned. In the garden of an older house, however, it can look quite attractive, especially if little pockets are left for plants. All sorts of alpine and rock plants can be grown in a crazy-paving path to make a strip of living colour.

If you can run to it, buy natural stone paving. Split York-stone is very attractive and because it can be obtained in quite thin pieces it is only a fraction of the price of natural rectangular paving. However, what you save on the cost of the paving you will lose again to some extent on the extra sand and cement necessary. Crazy paving must, in the main, be laid on a solid bed of mortar, so you will certainly need more sand.

Lay the base in exactly the same way as recommended for rectangular paving, using concrete if there is any chance of sinkage. Don't forget to put in the pegs for levelling. The mortar is made as for rectangular paving using a 3/1 mix of soft sand and cement.

Start by selecting a few larger pieces. These are laid first round the edges of the area to be laid. The largest pieces can be laid on five points of mortar but smaller lumps must be set on a solid bed. Remember that if you are using split, natural paving that has been cut quite thin, it will not take a lot of weight. So this, too, is best laid on a solid bed.

When laying the slabs, leave a space in between each

75

piece to allow for pointing in. Because the pieces are not of a uniform shape, the spaces will be irregular, but they should be made to fit as nearly as possible.

1. Lay large pieces with straight edges on the outside and fill in with smaller pieces, tapping them down level.

Once the outside pieces are laid, fill in the middle, selecting pieces at random. Now this is the bit that really does drive you crazy. Fitting the pieces together is rather like doing a jigsaw puzzle and it can be just as time-consuming. Don't even attempt to sort through the stack each time you need a bit to fit a certain place. Keep a club hammer and a chisel nearby, select a piece that nearly fits, and chop off the odd corner that is out of shape. Otherwise, you'll probably shift that stack of paving dozens of times before you're finished.

As before, keep the straightedge in use all the time to check levels. This is not as easy with natural paving as with artificial, because the stones do not have a smooth, regular surface. In this case, you will have to be content with a slightly less level surface. A little water will be bound to lodge on the top of natural crazy paving. I think it looks attractive, but if it worries you, you will have to make the overall slope a little sharper.

2. Check regularly that the individual pieces are level, and run the straightedge from the stones to the pegs.

Once the paving has set hard – generally after about two days – it should be pointed in. Don't attempt to do this job too early, or you will find that the pieces move as you tread on them and this will naturally upset the levels.

Pointing in can be done with soft sand, or if you want a stronger joint use sharp sand. Soft sand is perhaps better if you are using a natural stone, such as York, because it will better match the colour of the stone. Sharp sand looks greyer when set, and is therefore best to use with concrete or granite slabs.

3. The finished path should be pointed in with mortar and then 'lined out' for a really neat finish.

Mix the mortar as before, using a 2/1 mix of sand and cement and a bucket to measure the materials accurately. With crazy paving, the pointing cannot be done by brushing in a dry mix. Make the mortar fairly sloppy so that it will work well with a trowel. Place it on a spot-board near where you are working, and put it in with a small pointing trowel.

The mortar should be worked well down between he slabs with the edge of the trowel, and then smoothed to give a nice, clean surface level with the top of the stones.

The finish of the pointing is important, since this will set off the paving. There are two popular ways of finishing it off. Either the trowel is run down the line of cement at an angle so that it is raised slightly towards the middle, or it is marked out with lines. Lining out is done after the mortar has dried, but before it is set solid. Don't leave it too long, or you may find that it has set too hard.

Lining is best done with a stout piece of wire bent into a U shape. An ideal tool for the job is a bricklayer's butterfly. This is a piece of wire, shaped like a pair of butterfly wings, that is used to tie two walls together. Bricklayers use (and lose) hundreds of them in the course of building a house, so if your house is new you may well find several knocking about the site. If not, your friendly builder's merchant will no doubt be pleased to give you one.

When you do the lining out, you will probably find that it throws up small 'crumbs' of mortar that look rather unsightly. Don't worry about these. They will brush off with a soft brush the following day. If you have slopped a bit of mortar onto the stones, it will stain and look ugly. It can be removed by brushing the surface of the stones with a wire brush once the mortar is hard.

If there is any danger of frost, either put a drop of concrete anti-freeze into the mixing water, or cover the whole area with hessian or paper.

12 Bricks

Bricks make a very attractive path in most gardens, or they can be used infilled into rectangular paving to create an interesting texture pattern. They are also a very versatile medium, since they can be used in a variety of patterns to form squares or circles, straight lines to break the monotony of square paving, or in curves.

It is, however, essential to use the right kind of bricks. Never use ordinary fletton bricks or sand-faced flettons, such as those used to build walls. These are made specially to be used vertically, where water will run off them immediately. If they are used on the flat, water lies on them and

1. Bricks make an attractive and durable paving material, but you must be sure to choose the right types.

penetrates the brick. At the first frost the water will expand and the surface of the brick will flake. The only bricks that are suitable for paving are stock bricks or the very hard engineering bricks. Bought new, both types will cost a lot of money, but it is generally possible to pick up second-hand stock or engineering bricks from the demolition contractor much more cheaply. They will also be weathered and will look much more mellow and attractive.

To lay them, make the base in the same way as described for rectangular paving, not forgetting the level pegs. Like crazy paving, they should be set on a solid bed of mortar. Being small, they are slightly more difficult to level, though a certain amount of gentle undulation is often acceptable provided there is enough slope to take away excess water.

If the bricks are being used as an infill in paving, levelling is no problem. Set the paving first, leaving out a space where the bricks are to go. By simply placing the straight-edge from slab to slab, the bricks can easily be tapped down to the correct level. For larger areas, level pegs are used exactly as for rectangular paving.

Leave a space of about 13mm(½in) between bricks to allow for pointing. Inevitably, you will find that bricks have to be cut, but this is an easy matter with a brick bolster and club hammer.

When the paving is completed, it must be pointed. The best way to do this is to brush in a dry mix of sand and cement mixed in a ratio of 2/1. Again, make sure that the bricks are perfectly dry before doing this, and cover the whole area with about 2.5cm(1in) of soft sand before watering over the top in a fine spray. Afterwards, the sand is brushed off to leave a clean finish.

If you decide to lay bricks in a circle it is important to line them up properly so that the edge of each brick faces into the centre of the circle. Start by deciding on the size and position of the circle, and bang a stout peg into the centre. Tie a piece of string the length of the circle's radius to the peg, and mark out for the base. Set the concrete for the foundation, leaving the centre peg and the string in position. The edge of each brick can then be lined up, using the string. If your circle is round a tree (and this can look very attractive) the string must be looped rather than tied round the trunk so that it will move round it. Otherwise it will shorten as you move it round.

Cobbles

Cobbles are large round or oval stones, generally of granite. When set, they are naturally difficult and uncomfortable to walk on, so the siting of them must be planned carefully. Don't put cobbles in a place that will get a lot of use or where garden furniture is to be set up, since the surface will be very uneven. Indeed, they are often used specifically to discourage pedestrian traffic, in places where it is desirable to prevent people walking.

It is naturally impossible to level cobbles accurately, but since they are usually only used as infills in rectangular paving, this presents few problems.

Set them in sharp sand, again using the 3/1 ratio of sand and cement. They are set in rows, and tapped down individually with a club hammer. Make the mix fairly dry, or you will find that, as you tap down one stone, another already previously laid pops up.

Pointing of cobbles is impossible and unnecessary. All you need to do is to brush between them with a soft hand-brush when the mortar is getting dry, but before it gets hard. This will be sufficient to give a level enough surface. The mortar should finish about 2.5cm(1in) below the level of the tops of the cobbles.

Setts and stable blocks

Granite setts are generally cubes of stone, and are used particularly in road building. It is possible to buy them new, but second-hand setts are normally freely available and very much cheaper. It is now possible to buy concrete setts that are a very good imitation of the real thing, but very much thinner, and therefore even cheaper.

2. Cobbles can be used as an infill in rectangular paving or to discourage pedestrian traffic.

They, like bricks, are a very versatile medium because of their small size. They can be used as infills in paving, in straight lines, squares, rectangles or circles. They are laid in exactly the same way as bricks.

Stable blocks are made of the same material as engineering bricks, giving a dark grey, almost black finish. These are generally laid in a square pattern and look very attractive set in paving or on their own. It is possible to buy them second-hand, though they are quite difficult to come by. Alternatively, the same effect can be had by using block paving. This gives the same effect as stable blocks but is laid in exactly the same way as rectangular paving. Again, they are more expensive than normal paving, and are generally used as an infill.

To avoid the garish effect of white pointing with these dark coloured blocks, it is best to colour the pointing mortar with a grey cement colourant.

Paving blocks

A new concept in paving has recently been introduced with the express aim of simplifying the job for the do-it-yourselfer. Frankly, I wonder whether it is, in fact, easier to do than straightforward rectangular paving. But the end result is certainly very attractive and the problem of levelling is reduced to a minimum.

The system uses rectangular concrete blocks that look very much like bricks, except in colour. The area to be paved is first edged with wooden shuttering, which is levelled with a spirit-level. Soft sand is then spread inside the shuttering and levelled off by drawing a board backwards and forwards across the shuttering in much the same way as described for concreting. The blocks are then set out in a pre-chosen pattern on the sand. Don't tamp them down at this stage.

When the whole area has been laid, you will have to hire a vibrating pad. These consist of a machine with a large plate on the bottom. When the engine is started, the pad

3. Concrete blocks are easy to lay and can, like bricks, be set in a variety of patterns.

4. After laying, they are pointed with a dry mix, and consolidated with a vibrating pad.

vibrates rapidly backwards and forwards, pressing down the blocks evenly as it goes. The vibrating action makes a very strong job of firming the blocks – even stronger if you 'stabilise' the sand using a mixture of six parts sand to one of cement. If sharp sand is used instead of soft, the finished paving should be strong enough to take a car.

After vibrating, brush in a mixture of two parts sand to one of cement and go over it again with the vibrating pad. This will work the pointing mix down quite a bit, so the operation may have to be repeated to top it up.

13 Inspection covers

What garden is not 'blessed' with at least one inspection cover? I have seen new, small gardens with as many as five! They are necessary, of course, to allow access to drains and sewage pipes, so it is essential that they should not be covered with paving. The answer is to incorporate them into the paving and, with a little ingenuity, this is not as difficult as it sounds.

The problem is, that they are very rarely set in line with your paving and you will be very lucky indeed to find them set at the correct level. They will generally have to be raised or lowered so that the top of the cover is exactly level with the surface of the paving.

Unless the cover is so low as to be below the level of the concrete base for the paving, the area can be pegged level and the concrete put in first. If it is below the concrete level it will have to be raised first. It is possible to do the whole job before the paving is laid, levelling the top of the cover to the pegs, but I prefer to wait until the paving reaches the manhole. This way you could save yourself quite a bit of cutting round the cover.

Start by removing the lid. Old covers were equipped with metal lifting rings, but new ones generally have two slots at the ends, to take a special key. If you don't have a key, it is relatively simple to lift the cover by inserting a trowel between the cover and the frame and levering it up.

The frame will be cemented to the brickwork and this should now be removed. Before starting work, make sure that no-one in your family is likely to flush the lavatory or empty the bath, and place an old sack in the hole to catch any bits of mortar, and prevent the drain becoming blocked.

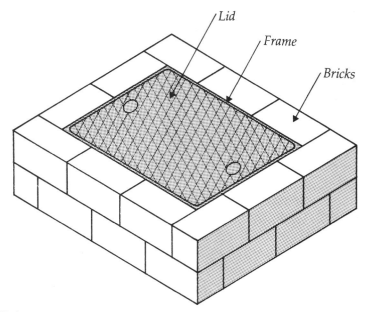

Lid

Frame

Bricks

To lower an inspection cover, remove the lid, chip out the frame and remove a course of bricks. Then refit the frame and replace the lid.

The frame can now be chipped away from the brickwork with a hammer and chisel. Take great care when you do this job, since the frames are made of cast-iron and will break easily. If you get it out intact you can re-use it, though if the cover is in a position where it will be run over by vehicles, you will have to change it anyway. Cast-iron covers in this situation must be replaced by steel ones, which are readily obtainable at the builder's merchant. If you expect heavy lorries to run over the cover you will have to go even further and buy a heavy-duty steel cover. Your merchant will be able to advise you.

With the cover and frame removed, it will be easy to see, using the straightedge across two pegs, how much you have to raise or lower the brickwork. You will almost certainly find that the distance is more or less than the thickness of a brick, and this will mean cutting. To cut a brick in half lengthways, the easiest thing to do is to cut off the 'frog'. This is the indentation in the top of the brick. With a brick bolster and club hammer it will come off quite easily and cleanly. You may even find that half a brick is too thick, and in this case you will have to use tiles or even slates.

Use a 3/1 mix of sand and cement to set the bricks, tiles or slates in place, bringing them up to just below the final level as shown by the pegs. Leave the setting of the frame until you have laid the paving right up to the manhole. The frame can then be set to line up with the paving. This will probably not quite line up with the brickwork, and will look somewhat messy. Not to worry, it won't be seen when the inspection cover is in place.

If you have to lower the cover, you will need to knock off the necessary rows of bricks, and may have to put in half a brick or a row of tiles to bring it up to the correct level.

If you want to make the inspection cover really unobtrusive, buy a 'Broads' cover. This consists of a metal frame into which concrete is set. The concrete can be coloured with a colourant powder to match the colour of the paving. When both the concrete and the paving get a little faded and dirty, it will be hardly possible to see the cover.

When the job is completed, make sure you remember to remove the sacking you placed in the hole, and clean it out well.

14 Walling

Walls fulfil many functions in the garden, and in most schemes some walling is desirable. Retaining walls in sloping gardens, boundaries, screens, flower boxes and features can all be built in stone or brick and will add height in an attractive way.

Brick or artificial stone is easier to use than natural stone (with the possible exception of trimmed York-stone) because of its uniform shape. With natural stone, however, because of its informal appearance, a certain amount of leeway in the levels is acceptable.

Brick walls

Bricks can be used in almost any situation. Naturally you should try to choose a brick that harmonizes with its surroundings. If possible, it is obviously desirable to use the same bricks as those used for the house walls, especially if the walling is to be near them. In an older garden, second-hand bricks look more mellow and make a very attractive feature. They can be bought from most demolition contractors. Never use common flettons outside. They are designed primarily for inside walls, and are likely to flake when frosted. If you use sand-faced flettons, note that they have three sides that are treated with a sand finish. It is these sides that are weatherproof, and only they should be seen.

Make the foundations as described previously, tamping down the concrete well and finishing it off so that the top surface is level.

The mortar is made with three parts by volume of soft

builders sand to one part of cement. It is advisable to use a special masonry cement, or to put a proprietary plasticizer in the mixing water. This will make the mortar easier to use, and it will also make the hardened mortar a little more plastic. This means that, if there is a slight movement in the wall due to alternate heating and cooling, the mortar will not crack. If you don't have a plasticizer, a few squirts of washing-up liquid will do much the same job. Make the mix fairly sloppy for bricks.

Again, as for paving, place a spot-board near where you are working to facilitate picking up the mortar. If the walling is next to a paved area, it is a good idea to put a shallow layer of soft sand over the paving near the wall. Any splodges of mortar that fall on it will not then stain, and can be picked up quite easily afterwards.

Start by laying the first brick at one end of a run. Set it with the frog (the depression in the brick) uppermost on a bed of mortar about 2cm(¾in) thick. Tap the brick down with your trowel until there is about 13mm(½in) of mortar under it. Then check it for level, both ways.

Next go to the other end of the run and repeat the process. You will now be able to stretch a bricklayer's line between the two. For the first row or two, I always wrap the line round a spare brick to hold it in place. For subsequent courses, use a bricklayer's line pin stuck in the mortar. Then check that both bricks are aligned. By sandwiching the line between a loose brick on top of the one you have laid, you will be able to position the line so that it runs exactly along the front edge of the brick. If the run is

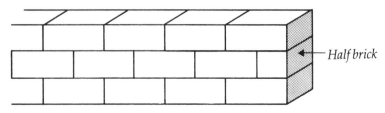

Fig 1. Bonding on a straight run.

very long, you may have to set one or two bricks temporarily in the middle of the run. Using the line as a guide for both line and level, you will be able to lay the first course.

Before butting each brick against the one you have just laid, place a splodge of mortar with the trowel on the two end corners. When the brick is pushed against the last one these two splodges will spread, and no pointing will be necessary afterwards. You may find that putting on the splodge of mortar is a bit of an acquired art, but with a little practice and the right consistency of mortar, you'll quickly get the hang of it.

The second row must be bonded over the first, so that the brick lies with its middle over a joint. If you are building the wall in one single straight run, this will necessitate starting and finishing each alternate row with half a brick.

If, however, you have two or more runs which are set at right-angles to each other, you should lay the first row of the second run before starting on the second course. Since a brick is exactly half as wide as it is long, it is therefore simply a matter of laying the first brick in the row crossways. The illustration makes it quite clear.

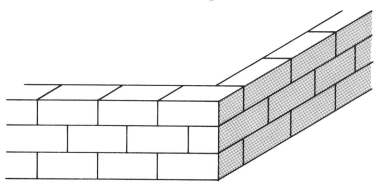

Fig 2. Bonding a right-angle.

As you progress up the wall, check with the spirit level that the bricks are level both ways, and also hold it against the front of the wall to make sure that it is going up straight.

When you reach the top of the wall, a coping must be provided to shed water. This can be done on double-thickness walls by placing a row of bricks on their sides across the wall.

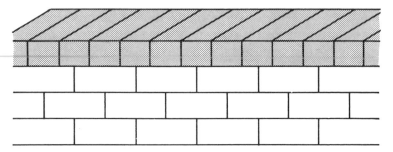

Fig 3. Coping on a double wall.

For a single wall, which is of course too narrow for this, use a special concrete or stone coping about 12.5cm(5in) wide. Set it so that 2.5cm(1in) projects over the face of the brickwork. Alternatively, buy a special bevelled coping which is set so that the apex of the bevel is in the centre of the wall, and projects over the brickwork about 2.5cm(1in) either side.

If the wall is being used to retain soil, it is important to leave weep holes in the first course, to allow water to get away from behind the wall. Otherwise it could soon push it down. Simply leave out half a brick at intervals along the wall, and set in a clay drainage tile. The tile is not in fact necessary, but makes a neater job.

When the mortar is dry but not hard, the wall should be pointed. In fact, with garden walls, it is not necessary to go to the lengths a bricklayer will go to when building a house wall. The simplest way is to wipe over the joints with a piece of wetted sacking to give a neat, flush joint.

Alternatively, cut off the end of a metal bucket handle and use this to rake out the mortar. It will give an attractive, modelled finish.

Taller walls

For a taller wall, for instance one over about 1m(3ft) high, a double row of bricks should be used. This is also necessary if you are using sand-faced flettons where both sides of the wall will be seen and exposed to the elements. Remember that the backs of these bricks are not faced and look ugly, apart from not being weatherproof.

Double walls are built in much the same way except that both sides are built together. The bond is then achieved by placing every other brick across the line of the run, giving much greater strength.

If you are building a tall retaining wall, it will have to withstand a lot of pressure, and here it may be worthwhile building a super-strong construction. This is made by building the two rows with a gap in between. The gap is then filled with concrete to give greater strength. Since the back of the wall will not be seen, this can be made with breeze or concrete blocks. It is as well to tie the two walls together with a builder's butterfly – the twisted wire tie described in the chapter on crazy paving.

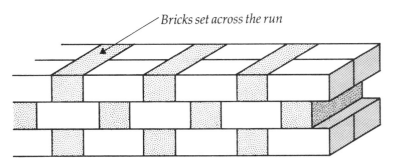

Fig 4. Bonding a solid double wall.

Stone walls

Though many of the techniques are similar for building stone walls, there are certain vital differences. This is mainly due to the fact that stone has a much rougher, more informal surface than brick. For this reason the mortar for stonework must be much drier than that used for bricks. If a little mortar drops onto the face of a brick it will generally fall off, or can easily be flicked off with the point of a trowel. On the rough face of stone it will stick like glue.

Because the mortar is drier, the stones will have to be tapped down with a club hammer, and it will be impossible to make a splodge of mortar stick to the ends as you would with brick. For this reason, it is necessary to point each row of stones before continuing with the rest.

But perhaps the biggest difference is that, because of the uneven face, it is impossible to check that the wall is going up straight by using the spirit level. Still, there are ways and means, and all will be explained later.

Facing stone

Both artificial and natural walling stone can be bought with either a 'cut' or a 'rock' face. A cut face leaves the front of the stone more or less flat, while a rock face makes the front project, giving a less formal and, in my opinion, more attractive finish. Rock-faced stone is more expensive than that with a flat face, because each stone has to be faced. However, it is quite an easy and satisfying job to do yourself.

Start by making a bench. If you have a lot of stone to face, it will be hard on the back if you try to do it crouching down. What you need is a bench that will allow you to work standing up. The ideal height is achieved by placing a paving stone on top of a forty-gallon drum. You should be able to pick one up from a garage or a factory for a pound or so. You'll also need a brick bolster, a club hammer and a straightedge. A straight piece of wood about 4cm × 13mm × 30cm(1½in × ½in × 1ft) is ideal.

Mark a line on the top of the stone, about 13mm(½in) from the face, and chip away the top edge of the stone. Now do the same on both ends, giving yourself a mark to make the line on the other side of the stone. Make sure that the lines chipped away on the ends of the stones are exactly at right-angles to the top, or the wall will not go up straight when you come to building.

1. Walling stone will look better if it is 'faced'. Start by marking a line 13mm (½in) from the face edge.

2. Using a brick bolster and club hammer, chip away the edge along the line you have marked.

95

3. Now repeat the process on the ends, making sure that the cut is at right angles. Then do the other side.

4. The foundations for the paving should be just a fraction below the level of the paving.

5. When mixing the mortar, make a 3/1 mix of soft sand and cement, using a bucket to measure the quantities.

6. Set the first stones at each end of a run, making sure that it is level with the spirit level.

7. Stretch a tight line along the edge of the stones and hold them in place with a loose stone on top.

8. Now set the remainder of the stones in the run, tapping them down so that they are level and in line with the line.

9. If the wall is to retain soil, weep holes must be left in the bottom course to allow water to escape.

10. If you decide to use 'jumpers', they must be set after the remainder of the course. Remove one stone.

11. The jumpers are made the same length as the stones but twice the height, so they will fit into the space.

12. The jumper must be levelled independently, making sure that it is perfectly level both ways.

100

13. Once the first course is laid, it must be pointed in with mortar before the second course is set on top.

14. The top of the wall should be finished with a coping stone which projects a little over the front of the wall.

15. When the mortar is dry but not hard, it should be pointed by raking it back with a short piece of wood.

16. If any mortar has fallen on the face of the stone, it should be removed afterwards, with a wire brush.

Building

When you are ready to start, set the first two stones at each end of the run, in the way described for bricks. The brick-layer's line is then set to run along the line you have cut when you faced the stone. As you set each stone, check with the spirit level that it is level both ways. This should ensure that the wall goes up straight, but it is worthwhile standing back and sighting along the wall after each run is set. If you have a good eye you will easily see any mistakes. If not, bang a straight stake at the end of each run, level it with the spirit level so that it is perfectly upright, and sight the wall against it.

When each course is laid, it will have to be pointed by working mortar in between the stones with the edge of a pointing trowel. Leave it rough at the front for the time being. When the wall is completed, or before you finish for the evening, the rough mortar at the face of the wall should be raked out with a piece of wood, to leave it recessed about 13mm(½in).

Some manufacturers will supply 'jumpers'. These are stones made twice the thickness of the main body of stones, and they should be set in the wall here and there to give an attractive random effect. To ensure that they don't interfere with the bricklayer's line, they must be set when the remainder of the course is finished, and levelled with the next course.

As with brickwork, the final job is to set a coping stone on the top of the wall. These can generally be bought with the walling, and are cut to size. If you have faced the walling stone, these will also have to be faced, and they should be trimmed so that each stone is exactly the same width. Again, set them so that the front of the coping over-hangs the wall.

Examine the wall carefully when you have finished. If there is any mortar stuck to the face, brush it off with a wire brush. It should come off cleanly if your mortar was dry enough.

Piers

Brick or stone walls can be simply finished 'straight' or they can be finished off with a pier. This provides a logical and definitive finish to a run of walling, and adds strength. For walls over about 1m(3ft) high, they should be considered necessary. Piers are also necessary if you intend to hang a gate in a run of walling. The constant use of even a small gate will place quite a stress on the wall. For added strength, the piers can be filled with concrete, or they can be left hollow, filled with a suitable compost and planted up to make an attractive feature.

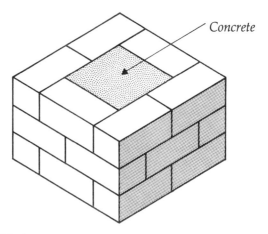

Fig 5. For added strength piers can be filled with concrete.

The dimensions of the pier should be such that constant cutting of bricks is eliminated. This means that the smallest pier will be 1½ bricks wide. This is really rather too small. A better size is 2½ bricks wide.

As with straight walling, make the foundation twice the size of the finished pier. Naturally, if the pier is to add strength to the wall, it must be built with it, so that the wall keys into it.

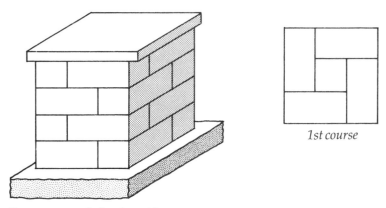

Fig 6. A pier 1½ bricks wide

1st course

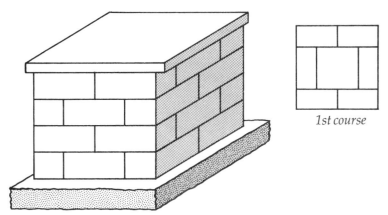

Fig 7. A pier 2 bricks wide

1st course

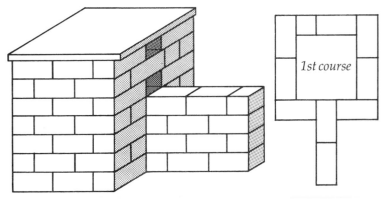

Fig 8. Keying a wall into the pier

1st course

105

The bricks or stones are set in much the same way as described for straight brickwork. The only difference is that, since the runs are too short to use a bricklayer's line, the stones are levelled in with a spirit level.

If you intend to hang a gate on the pier, don't forget to set the necessary fittings in the brickwork as you build.

Arches

The building of an archway should not be approached lightly. This is quite a skilled operation, but with care, the competent handyman can make a good job.

The brickwork forming the archway is fashioned around a wooden template, which supports the bricks until the mortar is hard, when it can be removed and the arch will be self-supporting.

Make the template as shown in the drawing, using stout timbers and hardboard or plywood. This is set up in the space left for the arch, and temporarily fixed to the brick-

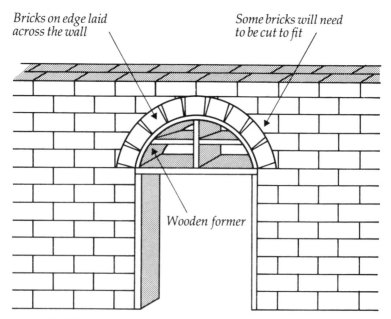

Fig 9. Building an archway using a wooden former.

work with nails driven into the mortar. Leave the nails projecting a little from the timber, so that they can be easily withdrawn when you remove the template.

When the curved part of the arch is reached, the bricks are set across the line of the brickwork, and on edge to give added strength. Building then continues normally, cutting the bricks in to meet the curve as you come to it.

It will be seen that this method of building is only suitable for walls 23cm(9in) wide, and will not work on 11.5cm(4½in) walls. Indeed, arches should not be attempted in walling less than 23cm(9in) wide.

Once the mortar is hard, the template can be removed and the arch will be self-suporting.

15 Steps

In steeply sloping gardens, steps are a necessity. But they should not be considered purely utilitarian. Well designed and built, they can make a very attractive feature in themselves. But, as with paths, they should never be skimped even if they are designed to be purely practical. If they are too narrow, or too steep, they will make the remainder of the garden appear smaller, upsetting the scale of the overall scheme. Obviously the width of steps will vary according to the design and size of the garden, but you should aim to make them at least 1.2m(4ft) wide.

The depth of the treads (the flat part of the step) should also be fairly generous – never less than 45cm(18in). The height of the risers – the upright part – will vary according to the difference in height between the lower and upper levels that the steps join. It is important, though, to make them neither too low, when they are un-noticeable and can constitute a dangerous 'trip', or too high, making them difficult and tiring to climb. Ideally, they should be 12–15cm(5–6in).

Before you start setting out the steps, some careful planning is necessary. You need to decide how many steps you'll need, and how high the risers must be. Start by determining the distance between the top and bottom levels. Get somebody to hold the straightedge at the top level, and make sure it is level with the spirit level. Then drop a tape from the bottom of the straightedge to the bottom level to ascertain the difference in height.

Each step is to be between 12 and 15cm(5–6in) high, so the distance between the two levels should be divided by this amount to give the number of steps required. For example, if the difference in height was, say, 41cm(16½in) three steps, each 13.8cm(5½in) high, would be required. If the treads are to be 45cm(18in) deep, then allowing for an overlap of 2.5cm(1in) on each step, they will take up 127cm(4ft 3in) in length.

Start building at the bottom of the flight. Put in a concrete foundation, and set on this a course of bricks or stone. The height of the foundation takes a bit of head scratching too. If the riser is to be 15cm(6in) high, and you are working with bricks and paving slabs, work it out like this. The slab is 5cm(2in) thick. Allow for 13mm(½in) of mortar underneath this, making 6.3cm(2½in). The brick is 7.5cm(3in) thick and this will need another 13mm(½in) of mortar underneath it, making 15cm(6in) in all. So, the concrete foundation should come flush with the bottom level. If you only wanted the riser to be 12cm(5in) high, you would have to drop the concrete foundation by 2.5cm(1in) below the bottom level.

1. Start by setting a single course of stone as the bottom 'riser' of the steps.

With the bricks set, you can now dig out behind them and fill in with concrete, to make a base for the paving slab treads. Set these on the bricks, leaving an overlap at the front of about 2.5cm(1in). At the back of the paving slabs,

2. When this is set, dig out behind it, low enough to allow a concrete base just below the level of the stone.

3. Using a dryish mix of ballast and cement, lay the base, making sure it is not above the riser level.

dig out the foundation for the second riser and make the second step in the same way. Bear in mind that, if the top step is to meet the lawn, the slabs should be a little below the grass level to allow for easy mowing.

4. Put a layer of mortar along the riser, and lay the slab on three mounds of cement mortar.

5. The slab should now be levelled so that it slopes very slightly towards the front.

6. Set the remainder of the slabs for the 'tread', and then fill behind them to form the base for the second riser.

7. This is now set just behind the first tread. The soil is then dug out behind and another step built.

16 Plants

However attractive your paving slabs may be, and however well they have been laid, they will still tend to look a little 'hard' in the garden setting. There's no doubt about it, hard landscaping of any sort needs plants to soften it. Chosen well, plants will also add a great deal of colour and interest to an otherwise barren area, and they will thrive with little or no attention.

Walls, too, can be brightened up with the addition of plants. It is quite surprising how little some alpine plants need for survival, and many will live happily stuck in a crevice in a wall, with no apparent means of sustenance. Not only will they grow – they'll thrive.

Obviously with paving, and walls too to a lesser extent, the place for planting must be carefully chosen. Leave clear the area that will get the most use. Plant those subjects that will put up with a little maltreatment where they may get trodden on or kicked, and leave the tenderer plants where they can enjoy a little peace and quiet to get on with their job.

Even without planting in the paving or walling, the area can be livened up with tubs and troughs of annual plants and walls can be decorated with pots and hanging baskets.

Obviously then, the first thing to do is to get to know your plants – which plants will do well, and where they will flourish. I have suggested a few here, but I would strongly recommend that you look out a good book on alpine and rockery plants and another on conifers before making your final choice. The great range of suitable plants is much too numerous to describe here.

Plants for crevices

Many alpine and rock plants can be grown in tiny crevices in walls and in paving. If you intend to plant a wall, leave a few spaces unpointed here and there and fill them with a little ordinary garden soil. They will also grow well in spaces left between natural paving. But if you wish to grow them between artificial slabs (which butt much closer together), simply chip off a corner where you want the plants to go, when you are laying the slabs. They will look unfinished and ugly until they are planted, but will reward your patience well when they grow. Work a little soil into the hole and push it down under the slabs. That will be plenty for most small plants.

Alyssum saxatile is the popular small, perennial alyssum. It is especially useful in walls, where it will tumble down, covering quite a large area. In the spring it is covered with a mass of bright yellow flowers. A common plant, but not to be scorned.

1. *Alyssum saxatile.*

2. *Aubrietia* on a wall.

Arabis, or rock cress, is another fairly common inhabitant of British gardens, and with good reason. It forms tufts of bright-green foliage covered in bright-pink or white flowers. A worthy plant for paved areas where it will not get a lot of rough treatment. This one can tend to get a bit straggly after a few years, so you may wish to replace it.

Aubrietia is another trailing plant that will do well in walls or in paving where it can be protected from pedestrian traffic. Again, it makes its show in the springtime, and its bright pink, blue, crimson, purple or lilac flowers make a striking contrast to *Alyssum saxatile*. This one, too, may get a little leggy after a few years and benefits from being trimmed back a little after flowering.

Potentilla aurea plena is a beauty for planting in paving, though it will not tolerate a lot of harsh treatment. It forms small hummocks of glossy green leaves that look bright and cheerful most of the year, but it is at its best in the spring, when it is covered with double yellow flowers.

The *Saxifrages* and *Sedums* are two very large groups of plants, most of which can be grown between paving slabs and in walls. There is a great variety of colour in these two families, but the foliage alone would warrant them a place. *Sempervivums* are another large group. Often known as houseleeks, they will live almost anywhere. I have seen dozens of them growing quite happily on tiled roofs where there is no apparent source of nourishment at all. They form rosettes of foliage that vary from the tiny, hairy spider houseleek to types with large, glossy, fleshy leaves. Their flowers too are varied, though even without flowers at all they make an attractive show and are a fascinating collector's plant.

Thymus, or thyme, is well known as a culinary herb, and of course can be planted in the paving to form a useful as well as decorative addition. But here again there are many, varied forms, with green, yellow, silver and variegated foliage and white or purple flowers. They can be planted where they will receive a little wear, because, when lightly bruised, they give off the most delicious, aromatic fragrance. Three distinct advantages with this family and definitely not to be missed.

3. *Sempervivum* growing from a wall crevice.

Larger plants

If you wish to grow larger plants in a paved area special provision will have to be made for them when laying the paving. In areas that will receive no use you can leave out quite large planting areas. These will add height and interest and will break up what may otherwise be a monotonous stretch of stone. Also, leave out the odd slab, or half a slab, here and there where taller plants will not be in the way.

When the paving has set hard, knock out the concrete base below the planting hole and fill it with compost (John Innes No. 3 potting compost is best). Don't use garden soil in the holes for the larger plants, since they will require better conditions than the alpines and rock plants. Of course, in larger areas left in the paving, almost anything will go, but in the isolated holes, conifers with a prostrate habit are definitely to be preferred.

There are several varieties of conifer that will grow very close to the ground and will spread along it, hugging the paving. These are ideal, because they can be trimmed back as you wish.

4. *Juniperus horizontalis.*

The junipers are probably the best of this type of low growing conifer, and there are several attractive forms.

Juniperus communis depressa, or Canadian juniper, forms a large, spreading mat of green stems and leaves, silver beneath and turning bronze in winter. It likes full sun and is one of the best for the purpose.

Juniperus communis effusa has green leaves, silvery beneath, and this one stays green in winter to make a pleasant contrast to the Canadian juniper.

Juniperus horizontalis, the creeping juniper, has a number of good forms, the leaves of which are greyish blue. Two of the best forms are *J.h.montana* and *J.h.wiltonii*.

Juniperus sabina has some useful forms for paving planting, though some of them will grow a little higher and should therefore be used only on larger areas. *J.s.cupressifolia* is a good, low-growing, green form, while *J.s.tamariscifolia* will grow a little higher, making a spreading, flat-topped bush of emerald green.

There are, of course, many other conifers and other types of plants suitable for growing in walls and paving. Generally, your local nurseryman will be able to advise.

5. *Juniperus sabina tamariscifolia.*

Growing in containers

One of the best ways of brightening up the patio, or that rather boring wall, is to grow plants in containers. With a collection of suitable containers, a succession of annual plants can be grown that will give colour through all the months of the year in which you are likely to use your patio. Fill them with annuals and keep moving them around to show them off to their best advantage. Of course, containers can be planted with perennials, but unless you use alpines and rock plants and a few dwarf conifers they never give the same amount of colour as do annuals.

Start by selecting containers that will suit the situation. Make sure they have adequate drainage holes and start filling by putting in a generous layer of drainage material. Broken pots, builder's rubble or gravel will all do the job. Then fill them with John Innes No. 3 potting compost. Don't use one of the newer soil-less composts, because they dry out too quickly and are difficult to water.

Start in the spring or early summer with summer bedding plants. Geraniums, fuchsias, petunias, salvias, alyssum and lobelia all look fine in containers. These are pulled out when the first frosts cut them down, and are replaced with spring bulbs, wallflowers, sweet-williams, pansies, forget-me-nots and the like. Try to avoid the taller growing plants, especially bulbs which have tender stems and will not stand up to exposure.

The same plants can be used in hanging baskets which can be fixed to walls with a hook plugged into the brickwork. Special 'half-baskets' are available and these are particularly suitable for walls.

The one golden rule with tubs, troughs and hanging baskets is 'Don't forget them'. Bear in mind that they will dry out faster than plants in the open ground, and the only source of water and food they have is what you give them. Forget them, and they will suffer quickly. Remember them, and they will reward you well.

17 Aftercare

One of the beauties of stonework is that once it's down it requires little or no maintenance. All that's needed for the most part is a broom! There are, however, one or two jobs to do occasionally in certain circumstances.

1. One of the advantages of paved areas is that most of the maintenance can be done with a broom.

However careful you may be with paving, it is quite likely that one or two slabs will 'rock' after a while. This is generally a fault in the laying, but even the best paviors are guilty of the odd one or two now and again. If the slabs have been butted up close together, it is almost impossible to lift them in order to relay. The cracks between the slabs are too small to allow a spade to be forced down between them to lift the offending slab. In this case the way out is to hammer a small wedge of wood between the slabs to prevent them rocking. Certainly, the wood will rot away in time, but by then enough dust and dirt should have worked down between the slabs to hold them firm.

Algae and moss will grow on damp stone, and this, although encouraged on garden walls because it mellows the brick or stone, is to be avoided on paving. Algal growth in particular will make the slabs slippery and potentially very dangerous. Both algae and moss are, of course plants, so they can be killed with an appropriate chemical. The cheapest is probably tar oil, used normally to kill overwintering eggs of insects on trees and shrubs. It is also very effective in killing moss and algae. There are also several proprietary formulations made specifically for the job, but these tend to be more expensive and no more effective.

Pointing in walls may become dislodged due to frost action. Here, the mortar must be raked right out of the wall to provide a 'key' for new pointing, and the space refilled with mortar made as before. Don't repoint when the weather is frosty or the new pointing will be affected in the same way.

Perhaps one of the biggest problems in paving is weed growth. No matter how closely the slabs are butted, or even if they are pointed in between, weeds, particularly grass, somehow seem to get a hold. It looks unsightly and can also be slippery. Though weeds can be scraped out with a knife, it is a laborious and time-consuming job, and will not prevent new seeds blowing in to start growing all over again. Undoubtedly, the best way to control weeds in paths and paving is by the use of chemicals.

2. Remove algae by watering with tar oil, and weeds with a weedkiller.

One of the cheapest chemicals to give total control of weeds in paving is sodium chlorate. But this has two disadvantages. Firstly, there is some fire risk, though the chemical is now generally sold with a fire-depressant in the formulation. More risk perhaps lies in causing damage to the plants that edge the paving. Sodium chlorate will 'creep' through the soil, and could well damage plants some way away from where it was applied.

Better are the newer total weedkillers which contain simazine. These will not only kill the weeds that are there, but will also prevent new seeds from germinating. Simazine will not 'creep' through the soil, but great care must be taken to ensure that it does not come into contact with the foiliage of plants you wish to keep.

The only other chore that will have to be seen to regularly is the feeding and watering of plants. Alpines and rock plants require very little fertilizer, and should be left alone unless they appear to be suffering. Conifers growing in spaces left in the paving will need feeding, and this should be done with a proprietary rose fertilizer early in the spring.

Plants growing in tubs, troughs and baskets will need regular watering. Generally, annual plants will need no feeding after they have been planted. All this does is to produce lush growth of the leaves and stems at the expense of flowers. A dressing of general fertilizer incorporated into the compost before planting will be sufficient, generally, to last them through their lives. Again, feeding should be carried out if the plants appear to be suffering.

3. Plants in tubs and troughs will need regular watering and feeding if they are to give of their best.

Glossary

Aggregate – A mixture of sand and gravel used to make concrete.

Algae – Tiny plants that grow on cold, damp places, forming a green slime.

Alpines – Plants that are native to mountain habitats.

Annual – A plant that is raised from seed, flowers and dies in the same year.

Bolster – A wide cold chisel used for cutting brick or stone.

Bonding – The practice of setting bricks so that joints do not correspond on alternate rows.

Butterfly – A wire frame shaped like a butterfly's wings, used to join two walls together.

Compasses – A drawing instrument used to make circles.

Coping – The capping of a wall used to prevent the entry of water.

Course – A row of bricks or stone in a wall.

Cure – To ensure that concrete dries slowly, giving added strength.

Damp-proof course (DPC) – A membrane of waterproof material set in a house wall to prevent rising damp.

Drainage tile – An earthenware pipe used for land drainage.

Engineering brick – A brick made of hard material used where excess loads are expected, or where frost would damage softer materials.

Face – The front of a brick or stone

Fat – A mixture of fine sand, cement and water, worked to the surface of concrete when tamped down.

Fillet – A narrow strip of cement left when pointing paving.

Fletton – A cheaply made brick used for interior walls.

Footings – Concrete foundations of a wall.

Former – A metal beam used for shuttering deep concrete.

French curve – A drawing instrument used for making curves.

General fertilizer – An artificial plant food containing the three major plant nutrients.

Gulley – An earthenware pot used to trap water and transfer it to the drainage system.

Hardcore – Any hard material, such as bricks or broken concrete, used in the base of driveways or paving.

Herbicide – A chemical weedkiller.

Inspection cover – The metal lid used to cover a hole made for inspecting drains and sewers.

Masonry cement – Special cement containing a plasticizer.

Mortar – A mixture of sand and cement used in bricklaying and paving.

Organic matter – Plant or animal debris that will rot down in the soil to form humus.

Perennial – A permanent plant that, though it may die down in winter, will flower year after year.

Plasterer's float – A wooden or metal float used to apply plaster.

Plasticizer – A cement additive that makes concrete more plastic and flexible.

Pointing – Filling in between bricks or slabs with mortar.

Portland cement – 'Ordinary' cement without additives.

Radius – The distance from the centre to the edge of a circle.

Random – An unplanned pattern of paving.

Retaining wall – A wall used to hold back soil.

Riven – Natural stone cut by hand, leaving a textured surface.

Roofing square – A large metal square used by roofers.

Sand-faced fletton – A cheap brick with a weatherproof face.

Sharp sand – A gritty sand used where strength is important.

Shuttering – A temporary retainer for concrete.

Soft sand – A soft, clay sand used for brickwork and paving.

Spirit level – A tool for ascertaining levels.

Stable blocks – Small, black, square blocks, traditionally used in stable yards.

Subsoil – The soil underlying the topsoil, generally not suitable for growing plants.

Weep hole – A hole in a retaining wall, allowing the escape of water.

Index